DISEASES AND DISORDERS

By Michelle Denton

Published in 2018 by
Lucent Press, an Imprint of Greenhaven Publishing LLC
353 3rd Avenue
Suite 255
New York, NY 10010

Designer: Andrea Davison-Bartolotta
Editor: Jennifer Lombardo

Cataloging-in-Publication Data

Names: Denton, Michelle.
Title: The Zika virus / Michelle Denton.
Description: New York : Lucent Press, 2018. | Series: Diseases and disorders | Includes index.
Identifiers: ISBN 9781534561298 (library bound) | ISBN 9781534561304 (ebook)
Subjects: LCSH: Zika virus–Juvenile literature. | Zika virus infection–Juvenile literature. | Communicable diseases–Juvenile literature.
Classification: LCC RA644.Z56 D46 2018 | DDC 614.5'885–dc23

Printed in the United States of America

CPSIA compliance information: Batch #BS17KL: For further information contact Greenhaven Publishing LLC, New York, New York at 1-844-317-7404.

Please visit our website, www.greenhavenpublishing.com. For a free color catalog of all our high-quality books, call toll free 1-844-317-7404 or fax 1-844-317-7405.

CONTENTS

Illness is an unfortunate part of life, and it is one that is often misunderstood. Thanks to advances in science and technology, people have been aware for many years that diseases such as the flu, pneumonia, and chicken pox are caused by viruses and bacteria. These diseases all cause physical symptoms that people can see and understand, and many people have dealt with these diseases themselves. However, sometimes diseases that were previously unknown in most of the world turn into epidemics and spread across the globe. Without an awareness of the method by which these diseases are spread—through the air, through human waste or fluids, through sexual contact, or by some other method—people cannot take the proper precautions to prevent further contamination. Panic often accompanies epidemics as a result of this lack of knowledge.

Knowledge is power in the case of mental disorders, as well. Mental disorders are just as common as physical disorders, but due to a lack of awareness among the general public, they are often stigmatized. Scientists have studied them for years and have found that they are generally caused by hormonal imbalances in the brain, but they have not yet determined with certainty what causes those imbalances or how to fix them. Because even mild mental illness is stigmatized in Western society, many people prefer not to talk about it.

Chronic pain disorders are also not well understood—even by researchers—and do not yet have foolproof treatments. People who have a mental disorder or a disease or disorder that causes them to feel chronic pain can be the target of uninformed opinions. People who do not have these disorders sometimes struggle to understand how difficult it can be to deal with the symptoms. These disorders are often termed "invisible illnesses" because no one can see the symptoms; this leads many people to doubt that they exist or are serious problems. Additionally, people who have an undiagnosed disorder may understand that they are experiencing the world in a different way than their peers, but they have no one to turn to for answers.

Misinformation about all kinds of ailments is often spread through personal anecdotes, social media, and even news sources. This series aims to present accurate information about both physical and mental conditions so young adults will have a better understanding of them. Each volume discusses the symptoms of a particular disease or disorder, ways it is currently being treated, and the research that is being done to understand it further. Advice for people who may be suffering from a disorder is included, as well as information for their loved ones about how best to support them.

With fully cited quotes, a list of recommended books and websites for further research, and informational charts, this series provides young adults with a factual introduction to common illnesses. By learning more about these ailments, they will be better able to prevent the spread of contagious diseases, show compassion to people who are dealing with invisible illnesses, and take charge of their own health.

A GROWING CONCERN

In mid-2015, a disease most people had never heard of burst onto the scene as the next in a long line of global epidemics. Headline news reported Brazilian babies being born with microcephaly, a rare disorder that slows fetal brain development and causes newborns to have tiny heads. The culprit? Zika fever, a quiet, unassuming illness that had been making its way across the Pacific Ocean from Southeast Asia—island to island—since 2007. Although some reports of birth defects had come from French Polynesia after Zika came and went, the two were never connected. It was only when the virus hit Brazil—and hit it hard—that microcephaly came into the spotlight as a possible side effect of Zika infection.

Since then, researchers have begun studying the virus and working to create a vaccine, but the general public has not been properly informed about how to handle the disease, and misinformation is everywhere. Some believe it is the end of the world—a disease that causes birth defects could wipe out the planet in a generation, they say. Others do not care at all; the world sees epidemics every other year, they reason, so it is a waste of time to worry.

The truth is that neither reaction is appropriate. Zika may be worrisome because of its lingering effects, but it is by no means a bringer of the apocalypse; it may be mild, but it could have serious consequences if ignored. Being aware is the most important thing during any epidemic, and Zika is no different in that regard.

What Is Zika?

Zika is a tropical virus, first found in Ugandan monkeys, that is spread mainly by mosquito bites. It generally does not cause any symptoms, making it very difficult to detect, and when it does cause symptoms, they are typically mild and easily confused with the symptoms of other diseases. So far, the latest strain has been found in North, South, and Central America; the Caribbean islands; Southeast Asia; the Pacific Islands; and Africa.

Zika is a flavivirus in the same family as West Nile, dengue, Japanese encephalitis, and yellow fever. They are predominately carried by mosquitoes and ticks, and they spread quickly and easily because these insects are everywhere. A paper published in 2014 hypothesized that flaviviruses came out of Africa with early humans during the first great migration about

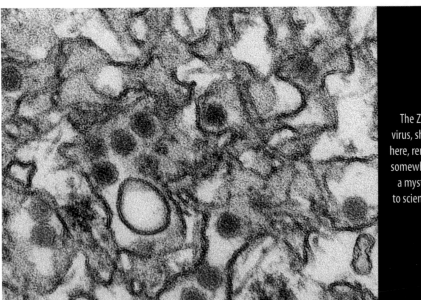

The Zika virus, shown here, remains somewhat of a mystery to scientists.

2 million years ago, making them some of humanity's oldest viral enemies. Zika was first diagnosed in 1952, but until 2007, cases of Zika infection were few and far between.

Both Mild and Severe

Generally, Zika's symptoms are mild, ranging from a fever to aches and pains to a rash. Only a few people have died of it, and in those cases, there were prior health issues involved that made the illness worse. Zika is not a deadly disease, but in rare cases, it can have dramatic, though nonlethal, side effects. Guillain-Barré syndrome (GBS), an unusual reaction to Zika, can cause muscle weakness and sometimes paralysis, and the birth defect microcephaly is being detected in unusually high numbers among the newborns of women who were infected with the disease while pregnant. These two complications are the main reasons why Zika has suddenly become such a hot topic.

Keeping People Safe

Even though protecting people, especially pregnant women, should be a top priority, organizations have been so blindsided by the disease that mounting a response has proven difficult and uneven. The U.S. government's response to Zika has been less than stellar. While certainly sympathetic to the people who have been affected, Congress has done more fighting among itself than it has against the disease while it decides how to fund measures to protect American citizens. The Centers for Disease Control and Prevention (CDC) has been attempting to educate the public to prevent people from being careless, but the media outshines its helpfulness with pieces that are meant to shock, not inform. Health departments across the country find themselves without resources to spread the word about Zika, leaving media outlets and Internet comments to do it for them, spreading misinformation instead. This means the responsibility for gaining awareness currently falls on the individual. The easiest way to protect oneself from Zika is to understand it.

CHAPTER ONE

ZIKA'S WORLD TOUR

Ayoung woman absently scratches at a mosquito bite on her arm as she wakes up to her alarm. She is mainly thinking about her visit to her doctor, which is scheduled for later that morning, and not the itchy bump that has been bothering her for about a week. At 10 weeks pregnant, she is barely showing, but already, she imagines the day she will hold her healthy baby in her arms. The only thing that overshadows her joy as she climbs out of bed is a slight pain in her joints and a mild headache to go with the fever she developed the night before. She dismisses them as symptoms of a flu bug she probably picked up at work and gets ready to face her busy and exciting day.

A few hours later, her world is turned upside down. She finds herself anxiously waiting to have blood drawn, her dreams of a happy, healthy baby shattered by the pamphlet on Zika that the doctor gave her, clutched tightly in her hand.

From its obscure origins in the jungles of Africa to the city streets of the United States, the Zika virus and its devastating effects on developing fetuses are emerging as a health crisis of global proportions.

Discovery in Africa

In 1942, Alexander John Haddow, a Scottish entomologist—a scientist who studies insects—went to Africa to study yellow fever, which is a virus transmitted to humans through the bite of an infected mosquito. For at least 250 years, the tropical and subtropical regions of Africa and South America had been plagued by the disease, and outbreaks in North America and Europe had also been common until the end of the 19th century. Although its symptoms are mostly mild, including fever, headaches, and muscle aches, yellow fever can also lead to hemorrhagic fever, which interferes with blood clotting, and jaundice, or liver damage, which causes yellowing of the skin and eyes and can sometimes be fatal. In the 1940s, mass vaccination efforts against the disease had begun, but the virus itself still required investigation. It was rightly believed that the disease had originated in African primates and had been carried to humans by mosquito bites, so Haddow and his team from the Yellow Fever Research Institute were capturing both monkeys and mosquitoes during their routine surveillance of the tropical Zika Forest near Entebbe, Uganda.

One day in April 1947, almost five years after Haddow's arrival, a captive rhesus macaque known as Rhesus 766 developed a fever at the Ugandan lab. Nonhuman primates do not typically exhibit symptoms when infected with yellow fever, so researchers took a blood sample from the monkey and injected

A rhesus macaque similar to this one was the first primate in Haddow's study to exhibit symptoms of what scientists now know was Zika.

it into the brains of lab mice. After 10 days, the mice became sick, and when studying their infected brains, the researchers discovered not yellow fever, but a new virus—one they had never encountered before.

The discovery did not seem to alarm Haddow. No mosquitoes had ever tested positive for the new disease—a fact that made him believe, at first, that it was a virus transmitted some other way. He also believed it was transmitted only among primates, since there had been no cases of human infection. In truth, even if there had been human cases at the time, they most likely went undocumented because the symptoms were so similar to those of a mild case of yellow fever that they were dismissed as either that or the common cold.

Haddow was more interested in the mosquitoes carrying yellow fever than a monkey with a new disease no worse than the flu. In order to study mosquitoes, the World Health Organization (WHO) funded the construction of a six-level wooden structure called Haddow's Tower, a tower in which "human bait"— local children—could stand at different elevations and attract mosquitoes for collection. Once a mosquito had landed and bitten, it was removed by researchers and put in a test tube for analysis. This went on for another year before, in 1948, an *Aedes africanus* mosquito carrying the same virus that had infected Rhesus 766 was caught and changed the game completely. Now, it was clear that the new virus was being transmitted among primates in the same way as yellow fever. There were still no human cases as far as anyone could tell, which made it more of a problem for primatologists—scientists who study primates, such as monkeys—and less of a problem for Haddow's team. However the previously unnamed disease was already evolving. As per protocol, the virus was named "Zika" after the forest where it had been found.

The Discoverer of Zika

Alexander John Haddow (1912–1978) studied zoology, or animal science, at the University of Glasgow in Scotland. He earned a bachelor of science degree in 1934 and a medical degree in 1938. He worked as a junior research fellow for three years before heading to Africa. In 1942, he joined the Yellow Fever Research Institute in Entebbe as an entomologist. It was there that he was part of the investigative team that discovered several viruses, including West Nile virus and Zika.

He was named director of the institute in 1953 and was awarded the Most Distinguished Order of St. Michael and St. George (Companion) in 1959 for his work there. This award, also known as a CMG, is a British order of knighthood given to British citizens who perform important work for the United Kingdom (UK) in a foreign country.

The First Investigations

Haddow and his colleagues George Dick and Stuart Kitchen published their discoveries about Zika in the *Transactions of the Royal Society of Tropical Medicine and Hygiene* in 1952. Since 1948, they had experimented on different kinds of monkeys, rats, guinea pigs, and rabbits, in addition to lab mice. In four different places in Uganda, humans had begun to be tested for the disease, too, and out of 99 Ugandans, 6 had antibodies in their systems to protect them against the Zika virus. Although the number was not entirely overwhelming, it suggested that their immune systems had come into contact with Zika and fought it off. None, however, were still infected when the tests were done.

After this initial report, many scientists went to work on Zika. It was only a little later in 1952 that the first active human case of Zika was documented. In Nigeria, which was a British colony at that time, the British health authorities were investigating an outbreak of jaundice, and a 10-year-old girl was brought to one of their clinics with a fever.

The Zika virus is named after the forest where it was discovered, which is sometimes spelled Ziika.

ZIIKA FOREST. PROPERTY OF UGANDA VIRUS RESEARCH INSTITUTE (UVRI) P.O. BOX 49 ENTEBBE TEL: 0414-720631

Although she did not have jaundice, a sample of her blood was taken, and in another lab mouse test, researchers discovered that she was carrying Zika. After six weeks, the girl had completely recovered, but medical science was still trying to find a place for her illness. Francis N. Macnamara, the director of the Virus Research Institute in Yaba, Nigeria, wrote a paper in 1954 focusing on the young Nigerian girl's case, but since his main question was whether or not Zika caused jaundice—which it does not—his report was wildly off-base.

Two years later, William Bearcroft, a new researcher in Macnamara's lab, volunteered for his own study and infected himself with Zika. He developed a headache and a light fever like the young Nigerian girl, but very little else came of his research. In an attempt to simulate the mode of transmission, he put *Aedes aegypti* mosquitoes, evolutionary cousins to the *Aedes africanus* mosquito that was originally found to carry Zika, on his arm and allowed them to bite him. He then tried to infect lab mice with the disease through the mosquitoes, but it did not work. All he had confirmed, in the end, was that Zika could, without a doubt, also be a human problem.

Almost a decade passed before someone else stepped forward with more reliable information. That someone was David Simpson, and in 1964, he claimed that neither the Nigerian girl nor Bearcroft had been the first human cases of Zika and that they had instead been sick with Spondweni, a related virus. The truth, according to Simpson, was that he himself was the first clinically studied Zika patient, having only recently recovered from Zika after contracting it while studying the disease in Uganda. Antibody tests confirmed that he had, indeed, had Zika, although his claims of being the first to have it remain unproven. What was unique about his symptoms, however, was that he was the only one of the first three documented cases—the Nigerian girl, Bearcroft, and Simpson—to have developed the telltale rash that often emerges with Zika infection. The pink rash, which was flat with raised bumpy areas, was spread out over Simpson's body. It covered his face, neck, torso, and arms, down to his hands, and it eventually appeared on the soles of his feet. Not painful or itchy, the rash lasted for five days, and Simpson described it as mild. This was a new trait of the disease, but a rash and a fever made Zika now look like dengue fever, another mosquito-transmitted virus common in tropical environments, which made it unlikely to be properly diagnosed by a doctor. In fact, for almost half a century, Zika was practically never documented, and while its spread through Africa and equatorial Asia was noted as cases cropped up here and there, it was never seen as a serious health threat.

Island Outbreaks

Through the turn of the century, scientists and doctors underestimated Zika because it was not causing major damage like the diseases it often mimicked; yellow fever, dengue, and West Nile virus were actually harming and sometimes killing people. Zika remained mild, and before 2007, only 14 active cases of the unassuming disease had ever been documented. In 2007, however, things began to change in the Pacific Ocean.

Yap Island, part of the Federated States of Micronesia, is a tiny island in the North Pacific Ocean that measures only 15 miles (24.1 km) long and 6 miles (9.6 km) at its widest point. Like the tropical forests in Africa and equatorial Asia, Yap is hot and rainy, averaging about 81 degrees Fahrenheit (27 degrees Celsius) and getting 120 inches (305 cm) of rain annually. In April 2007, it was the site of the first Zika outbreak in history, as well as the first place outside of Africa and Asia where the disease had been found. Doctors began reporting an "illness characterized by rash, conjunctivitis, subjective fever, arthralgia, and arthritis."[1] Conjunctivitis is better known as pinkeye; "subjective fever" means the person feels feverish even though a thermometer does not register a high body temperature; arthralgia is joint pain; and arthritis is inflammation and stiffness in the joints. While three people tested positive for dengue, which also causes rash and fever, 49 people were diagnosed with Zika, and another 59 cases were suspected but not confirmed. After a study of the island that included surveys and blood tests, researchers estimated that about three-fourths of the population, or 5,000 people, had actually been infected. Oddly enough, no mosquitoes carrying the virus were found in the area. However, it has since been determined that Zika can be passed on through sexual intercourse or a blood transfusion. It was suspected that an infected human may have travelled to the island or that an infected mosquito may have been brought in with an import, but no definitive cause for the outbreak was ever determined.

In April 2007, Yap Island (shown here) was the site of the first Zika outbreak in history, as well as the first place outside of Africa and Asia where the disease had been found.

A few isolated infections cropped up over the next few years. "Two U.S. scientists diagnosed in Colorado were apparently infected in Senegal," Jon Cohen summarized in an article for *Science*, a publication by the American Association for the Advancement of Science, "and one of them infected his wife, presumably through sex, when he returned home ... A U.S. Navy research station in Cambodia detected a case in a 3-year-old boy. A 52-year-old woman in Australia was diagnosed after returning home from a holiday in Indonesia."[2] Unlike the outbreak on Yap, which seemed to have come from nowhere, all of these cases originated in previously affected areas. The next outbreaks, however, were as unpredictable as the first.

From 2013 to 2014, Zika travelled around the South Pacific, particularly in the Oceanic region on the islands near Australia. At first, it was believed to be an outbreak of dengue, but many patients had already had dengue in their lifetimes, making it incredibly unlikely that they would catch it again. Instead, French Polynesia, New Caledonia, the Cook Islands, and Easter Island all found their populations in the midst of a Zika epidemic, with more than 11,000 people confirmed to have been infected and more than 30,000 medical consultations suspected of being due to the virus. It was quite obvious that Zika was being transmitted one way or another from countries such as Cambodia, Indonesia, Malaysia, the Philippines, Thailand, and Vietnam in Southeast Asia, where the disease is considered common. However, like the Yap Island outbreak, a definite source or a "patient zero" could not be found. Zika seemingly left Oceania as quickly as it arrived, and there has not been a confirmed case of it in French Polynesia since April 2014. Some suspect that Zika may still be circulating in the area but believe that since it is such a mild disease, infected people are not going to the doctor despite their symptoms. No matter the reason, Zika went quiet again, with only a handful of cases in the span of about a year before it arrived in Brazil.

Zika Crosses an Ocean

After 4 months and almost 7,000 cases of a strange, rash-causing sickness that was not dengue, chikungunya, measles, rubella, or any of the other more commonly seen diseases, the National Reference Laboratory in Brazil reported the first Zika outbreak in the Americas on May 7, 2015. On the same day, the WHO issued an alert about Zika virus infection, and suddenly, Zika was front-page news. A couple of years before, after the outbreak in French Polynesia, scientists had begun to draw loose connections between Zika and neurological disorders in both adult patients and babies born to mothers who had been infected right before or during pregnancy. Although no link had been established medically, the possibility of a disease that could affect the brain, especially the developing brain of a fetus, made people nervous. As with mad cow disease, bird flu, swine flu, and any number of other widespread epidemics, the media began regarding Zika as a possibly world-ending pandemic even though no one had ever died from it.

Although the first outbreak of Zika in Brazil was reported in May of 2015, it is believed that it was most likely brought in sometime around mid-2013.

Although previously thought to have been brought into the country by an international fan during soccer's FIFA World Cup or a championship canoe race, both held in Brazil in 2014, Zika was most likely brought in sometime around mid-2013. This new estimate suggests that Zika was in Brazil for almost a year before any cases were reported and that it was most likely transmitted around the end of the outbreak in the Pacific Islands, possibly by only a single person. "The introduction of one Zika virus leading to a widespread outbreak may seem surprising," observed Martin Hibberd, professor of emerging infectious diseases at London School of Hygiene & Tropical Medicine. "However, the modeling of other Zika outbreaks, and also the highly-related Dengue outbreaks, suggest that this is not unusual. In the right conditions, with sufficient mosquitoes and closely packed humans, the virus can spread rapidly."[3]

The 2016 Rio Olympics

Because Zika was suspected to have spread to Brazil during the FIFA World Cup, many athletes were concerned about traveling to Brazil for the Summer Olympics in 2016. Not only did they not want to bring Zika home in general, some refused to go for fear of infecting their partners when they came home. Several major champions declined offers to go, including Tejay van Garderen (cycling), Jason Day (golf), and LeBron James (basketball).

While these were reasonable fears, zero cases of Zika were reported after the Olympics, as most predictive models assumed. This, of course, does not mean that no one was infected. Since Zika does not show symptoms in most people, some most likely were infected, but the athletes who pulled out of the games were considered by some to be overly cautious.

Spread rapidly it did. By October 2015, Colombia, Mexico, Guatemala, Paraguay, and Venezuela reported cases of Zika, and by February 2016, Puerto Rico and a number of Caribbean islands, including the Bahamas, Haiti, Jamaica, and Martinique, had joined the list of infected areas. Puerto Rico's cases, in particular, frightened Americans because Zika had finally come to U.S.-owned land. While vacationing Americans had brought the disease back to the United States with them over the years, those cases had been isolated incidents acquired by travel and had not spread. In Puerto Rico, however, the virus was being locally acquired and actively spread around the territory by *Ae. aegypti* mosquitoes and human sexual activity.

On July 29, 2016, Florida announced the first locally transmitted Zika cases in the United States. As on Yap Island, no mosquitoes were found carrying the disease, but the Florida Department of Health stated in its report, "While no mosquitoes trapped tested positive for the Zika virus, the department believes these cases were likely transmitted through infected mosquitoes in this area,"[4] and this statement was backed by the CDC. Since then, 210 local cases of

Zika have been documented in Florida, and 6 have been documented in Texas.

In addition to its hop across the Pacific Ocean, Zika claimed its first life in July 2016. An elderly man in Salt Lake City, Utah, died after contracting the disease in Mexico. Although he had previously undergone treatment for prostate cancer, doctors reported that they believed Zika was the primary cause of death. The cancer treatment was considered successful, and the man had been healthy before being infected with Zika. However, his case made doctors consider the possibility that previous infection with a disease such as dengue, which the Utah man had before, might make Zika lethal even though it was generally quite a mild illness.

Later that year, in August, a Puerto Rican man in his late 30s died of GBS, which is a rare side effect of the Zika virus. GBS is even more rarely lethal than Zika. Although authorities did report that the man was obese, which may or may not have had an effect on his reaction to the disease, his relatively young age was what prompted state epidemiologist—a scientist who studies disease—Brenda Rivera to encourage caution. "What does this tell us?" she asked in an official statement. "That all of us are susceptible."[5] These two deaths, however, are the only confirmed cases of Zika having a fatal outcome, as of 2017. At the moment, it remains a very mild disease.

The Secret to Success

Zika's rapid spread is due largely to its ability to mutate. Viruses, in general, are constantly changing due to genetic mutation, and RNA viruses such as Zika are more likely to mutate than DNA viruses. As Chelsey Coombs of *The Atlantic* explained,

> *The flaviviruses' ability to spread so rapidly is also due in part to the structure of its genetic material.*

All viruses contain either RNA (short for ribonu-
cleic acid) or DNA [deoxyribonucleic acid]; flavivi-
ruses have a single strand of RNA that contains all
the information the viruses need in order to make
copies of themselves, which also means they mutate
more easily. Mistakes in replication can happen in
both DNA and RNA, but DNA has more systems
in place to proofread and correct mutations that
may naturally arise.[6]

Mutation occurs during a virus's reproductive phase, when an error is made in the genetic code of the next generation as the virus replicates. Sometimes, mutations have no effect, and other times, they have a negative effect, making certain virions—the part of a virus that transmits genetic code to host cells—less effective. Virions with negative mutations, however, generally do not survive to reproduce and pass along unfavorable traits. In other cases, though, it only takes one successful mutation in one virion to change the structure of the whole virus, creating a new strain that is better at infecting new hosts and more difficult for the immune system to fight off.

Researchers have found two different lineages for Zika, one from Africa and one from Asia, and overall, they have identified 41 strains of Zika. As the virus spread from African mosquitoes to Asian humans, a key protein shifted, suggesting that the structure of the virus changed to make it more effective when infecting humans. "All contemporary human Zika strains share a genetic sequence more similar to the 1966 Malaysian strain than the 1968 Nigerian strain," a University of California, Los Angeles (UCLA) study stated. "This implies the strains causing the current human outbreak evolved from the Asian lineage."[7] From this, it is easy to infer that the Asian strain's effectiveness on humans in particular is what brought it across the Pacific Ocean. Mosquitoes rarely travel so far, but humans travel all over the world, and a mutation that causes a disease to easily infect humans through human contact—in Zika's case, through sexual contact—is a very advantageous one. Mosquito-transmitted diseases have never before developed any other way to spread, making Zika both frightening and unique in its ability to mutate.

With Zika's unique ability to be passed not only by mosquitoes but through human sexual contact as well, it quickly grew from localized outbreaks to a worldwide health issue. Some travelers bring the disease home with them when they return from vacation.

Mutations may also explain the shifting variety of symptoms attributed to Zika. When it was first discovered in Africa, Zika's only apparent symptoms were fever and aches, and there was no evidence of neurological disorders in either adults or newborn babies like there has been in recent outbreaks. Then, the rash emerged in David Simpson's case, a symptom that would become a telltale sign of Zika but was then new—so new, in fact, that Simpson claimed to be the first clinically observed carrier of the disease even though it is likely that two others had it before him. Even later, in Micronesia, conjunctivitis and joint pain became symptoms, and neurological side effects in adults and newborns only began to emerge once Zika hopped to French Polynesia. Unfortunately, the current epidemic is most closely related to the strain from French Polynesia, making GBS in adults and birth defects in the children of infected mothers a rare but very real possibility in the Americas. Already, many newborns have been delivered with microcephaly, a condition that causes abnormal brain development. Doctors are still searching for more effective ways to detect Zika early—a task that has proven difficult because of Zika's mild nature and misleading similarities to other diseases.

CHAPTER TWO

SYMPTOMS, COMPLICATIONS, DIAGNOSIS, AND TREATMENT

Zika is a master of disguises. Sometimes, it produces only mild symptoms, such as a headache and joint stiffness, that mimic the common cold. Other times, it comes on like a flu or another kind of infection, with a fever, pinkeye, or a rash, clearly indicating that something is wrong. At still other times, Zika is so stealthy that there are no symptoms at all to show that it has made it past the body's defenses.

Zika can be asymptomatic, meaning without symptoms. However, even when symptoms are present, they are often so similar to those of other diseases that a test may be the only way to determine whether someone has been infected. Since the virus itself is relatively mild on its own and there are no lingering side effects for the host to deal with, it may seem unnecessary to test at all. Unfortunately, the havoc it can wreak on the brain and nervous system of a fragile new life makes testing vital for pregnant women, those who hope to conceive, and their partners.

Simple blood or urine tests can determine whether a person has, or has been exposed to, the virus. While there is no cure at present, if a person is found to either be infected with the virus or possess antibodies, steps can be taken to ensure that the next generation is kept safe from Zika-related birth defects.

Like the Flu

If an individual is among the few who experience symptoms when infected with Zika, the mildest of Zika symptoms they could have are fever, headache, and body aches. All of these, however, are also symptoms of influenza. "The public runs the risk of mistaking Zika for the flu," reported Samantha Olson of *Medical Daily*, "but knowing the characteristics of each condition is key to prevention and further infection."[8] In contrast to Zika, the flu also causes cough, sore throat, runny or stuffy nose, and sometimes vomiting and diarrhea.

Health officials caution against confusing Zika and flu symptoms. While they do share similarities, the flu is much more often lethal than Zika and should not be considered mild. In the case of fever, headache, or body aches, the infected individual should monitor their other symptoms and consider their recent history to discern a possible illness. Have they developed a rash, or are they coughing and sneezing? Have they travelled to a known Zika-infected area, or have they remained local? In either case, if any symptoms worsen, medical attention should be sought out.

The mildest symptoms of Zika are fever, headache, and body aches, and they are often confused with the flu.

Sore Eyes and Joint Pain

In addition to flu-like symptoms, Zika sufferers may also experience eye infections and swollen joints. Conjunctivitis, also known as pinkeye, is a common side effect of the Zika virus. Pinkeye is the inflammation of the thin, transparent tissue layer that lines the inner eyelid and the whites of the eyes, and it can cause itching, burning, swollen eyelids, and increased tear production, as well as the pink discoloration it is nicknamed for. Viral conjunctivitis, such as the kind that

Conjunctivitis is a common side effect of the Zika virus.

accompanies Zika, may also cause watery discharge. Zika infection may also come with eye aches that are unrelated to conjunctivitis.

Joints in the wrists, knees, ankles, fingers, and toes may also become swollen and painful to move. Some diseases, such as Zika, cause reactive arthritis by triggering an exaggerated immune system response. White blood cells are sent everywhere in the body to help fight the infection, but increased blood flow combined with the chemicals carried by white blood cells to help repair damage can cause inflammation and stiffness in joints. Logically, then, most Zika-related joint pain begins after the body had started to heal, although it can make it feel as if the disease is getting worse.

The Telltale Rash

One of the defining features of Zika is the rash that occurs on about 90 percent of people who show symptoms. The Zika rash is generally maculopapular, a very specific kind of rash. "The term maculopapular," explained Dr. Heather Brannon, "is used to define a rash that contains both macules and papules. A macule is a flat discolored area of the skin, and a papule is a small raised bump."[9] Typically beginning early in a Zika infection, the maculopapular rash is flat and pink, takes up a large area, and is covered in small red bumps. It starts on the face and moves downward, spreading to the upper body, arms, and eventually, the legs, hands, and feet. It may be itchy but is generally not; it is more likely to be mildly uncomfortable or feel hot, as if the skin is burning.

Like the joint pain that is common with Zika fever, the rash is generally considered to be a product of the immune system overreacting to the virus. While uncomfortable, it is not dangerous, and Zika cannot be transmitted by skin-to-skin contact even if a rash is present.

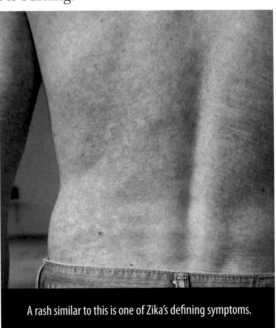

A rash similar to this is one of Zika's defining symptoms.

Guillain-Barré Syndrome

Although serious side effects from Zika are very rare, they do sometimes happen. The CDC describes GBS as a "sickness of the nervous system in which a person's own immune system damages the nerve cells, causing muscle weakness, and sometimes, paralysis."[10] It begins with a "pins and needles" feeling in the legs and feet, followed by weakness that eventually spreads to the upper body and peaks after about two to four weeks. Some may have difficulty walking or climbing stairs, as well as difficulty with eye and facial movements such as speaking, chewing, or swallowing. In severe cases, patients have displayed a loss of bladder and bowel control, rapid heart rate, unusually high or low blood pressure, and difficulty breathing. Sometimes, the muscle weakness can evolve into full paralysis, but most people recover within two to four weeks once the weakness levels out. Only 3 to 5 percent of GBS sufferers die from complications, among the most common of which are lung paralysis, blood clots, and heart attack.

Diagnosing GBS can be tricky since its symptoms are similar to those of a number of other neurological issues. In order to correctly diagnose the syndrome, doctors may use one or more of three methods: spinal tap, electromyography, and nerve conduction tests. A spinal tap, or lumbar puncture, involves the withdrawal of fluid from the spinal canal in the lower back. Commonly, when a patient has GBS, their spinal fluid changes, allowing doctors to properly diagnose them. In the event that the spinal fluid does not change, however, electromyography and nerve conduction studies may be used instead. During electromyography, tiny electrified needles are inserted into the muscle and measure the amount of nerve activity that occurs when an electric current is passed through it. Nerve conduction studies are very much the same except that the electrodes are taped to the skin rather than inserted, making them less invasive.

There is no cure for GBS, but certain treatments may speed recovery. Plasma exchange, in which the liquid part of the blood is removed to force the body to produce more, and immunoglobulin therapy, in which antibodies from blood donors are injected into a patient, are both commonly used to treat GBS. The goal of both treatments is to protect the body from the antibodies that have turned against the host and begun attacking the nervous system—one by removing the damaging antibodies and the other by protecting against them using healthy antibodies. Pain medication and blood thinners may also be used during treatment for GBS to prevent discomfort and blood clots from inactivity. Physical therapy is often administered as well to keep muscles strong and flexible.

In the United States, only about 3,000 to 6,000 people, or about 0.2 percent of the population, develop GBS per year, and only a handful of those cases have been said to be related to Zika. Although it is most commonly triggered by a respiratory or digestive infection, there is no exact known cause of GBS, and because of this, it was initially difficult to say whether or not Zika was involved. Only recently has GBS been connected to Zika by doctors around the world. In many countries, the incidence of GBS has increased since the Zika virus was introduced there. The WHO reported this increase in Brazil, Colombia, the Dominican Republic, El Salvador, French Guiana, French Polynesia, Guadeloupe, Guatemala, Honduras, Jamaica, Martinique, Puerto Rico, Suriname, and Venezuela. The WHO also noted that while no increase in GBS has occurred in places such as Bolivia, Costa Rica, Grenada, Haiti, Mexico, Panama, and Saint Martin, there have still been reports of Zika-related GBS that fall within the average number of cases of the syndrome per year. In a letter to the *New England Journal of Medicine*, analysts clearly spelled out the correlation:

> *During the weeks of ZIKV transmission, there were significant increases in the incidence of the Guillain–Barré syndrome, as compared with the pre-ZIKV baseline incidence, in [Brazil] (an increase of 172%), Colombia (211%), the Dominican Republic (150%), El Salvador (100%),*

Honduras (144%), Suriname (400%), and Vene-zuela (877%). When the incidence of ZIKV disease increased, so did the incidence of the Guillain–Bar-ré syndrome. In the six countries that also report-ed decreases in the incidence of ZIKV disease, the incidence of the Guillain–Barré syndrome also de-clined. When the seven epidemics of ZIKV disease are aligned according to week of peak incidence, the total number of cases of ZIKV disease and the Guillain–Barré syndrome are closely coincident.[11]

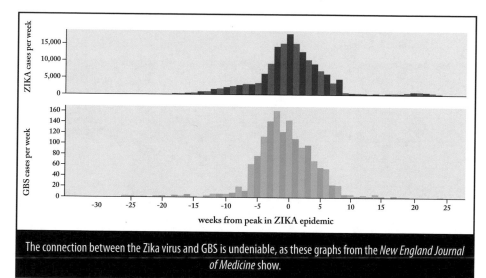

The connection between the Zika virus and GBS is undeniable, as these graphs from the *New England Journal of Medicine* show.

Although Zika is infectious, GBS is the only seri-ous health risk it poses for adults, and the odds of hav-ing it triggered by Zika in the first place are very low. The real threat Zika poses is for developing fetuses, and that is what makes it such a concerning disease.

Microcephaly

First observed in Brazil in 2015 and retroactively discovered during French Polynesia's Zika outbreak in 2013 and 2014, birth defects affecting the central nervous system (CNS) of newborns have been linked to the Zika virus. If infected with Zika during the first trimester of pregnancy, expectant mothers may pass the disease on to their fetus, an event that may cause developmental issues both in utero (during pregnancy) and after birth. As of January 2017, 29 countries and territories around the world have reported CNS malformation cases, including Brazil, Colombia, the United States, the Dominican Republic, Martinique, French Guiana, Guatemala, Bolivia, and Puerto Rico. The risk of microcephaly in newborns of women who contracted the disease during the first trimester is somewhere between 1 and 13 percent, depending on the area researchers are focusing on, making it a real but rare threat.

A fetus infected with Zika during the first trimester is at higher risk of developing a number of birth defects. The most common is microcephaly, which can be identified by a head that is smaller than normal and irregularly shaped.

Most common among the Zika-related birth defects is microcephaly. Babies born with microcephaly have abnormally small heads, a physical symptom of their stunted brain development. "During pregnancy, a baby's head grows because the baby's brain grows," explained the CDC. "Microcephaly can occur because a baby's brain has not developed properly during pregnancy or has stopped growing after birth."[12] In severe cases, a baby's forehead may even slope backward. While some grow up within normal ranges of intelligence and development despite their small heads, others may experience developmental challenges. The Mayo Clinic lists speech and movement delays, difficulties with coordination and balance, dwarfism, facial distortions, hyperactivity, intellectual disability, and epilepsy as some complications that could occur for children born with microcephaly. Cerebral palsy, hearing loss, and vision problems are also possibilities. Severe microcephaly is part of what doctors call congenital Zika virus syndrome, a specific pattern of developmental defects. Other symptoms include decreased brain tissue, damage to the back of the eye, joints with a limited range of motion, and muscle tone that makes body movement difficult.

Other Causes

While microcephaly in infants is one of the hallmarks of the Zika virus, the condition can also arise for a number of other reasons. Microcephaly is a neurological condition in which an infant's head is significantly smaller than normal, based on an average range for age and sex. It is generally the result of abnormal brain development while in the uterus, but it can also be caused by events after birth. While it may be genetic, other factors could include craniosynostosis, or the premature fusing of the joints between the bony plates of the skull; chromosomal abnormalities such as Down syndrome; decreased oxygen to the fetal brain due to complications during pregnancy or delivery; an infection such as toxoplasmosis, rubella, or chicken pox; or exposure to certain chemicals, drugs, or alcohol.

Unfortunately, there is no cure for microcephaly. It is a lifelong condition, but it can be managed with early intervention services such as speech, occupational, and physical therapies, as well as with medications to treat seizures and other health problems. In order to avoid the risk of microcephaly altogether, women who are pregnant—especially if they are in the first trimester, when the fetus is the most vulnerable—and women who might become pregnant should not travel to Zika-infected areas if they can help it. In Zika-infected areas, governments and communities are being encouraged to support local women in making informed decisions about pregnancy, although conversations about sexual and reproductive rights are sometimes difficult to start in predominately Catholic countries.

Miscarriages and Other Birth Defects

Microcephaly is not the only way in which unborn babies can be affected by Zika. Miscarriages (the death of an unborn baby), calcifications (abnormal buildup of calcium) in a baby's brain, babies being born much smaller than normal, and brain hemorrhages (bleeding in the brain) were some of the birth defects observed in a study by the Oswaldo Cruz Foundation in Rio de Janeiro, Brazil. Researchers followed 125 women who had been infected with Zika during different stages of their pregnancies, trying to figure out not only what birth defects are happening but how likely they are to occur depending on when a person is infected. The results were as follows:

- Infected during the first trimester, 55 percent had complications.
- During the second trimester, 51 percent had complications.
- During the third trimester, 29 percent had complications.

Researchers were at first hesitant to say that Zika causes birth defects and instead, generally suggested that they were merely linked. Mounting evidence, however, changed that. For example, until 2015, reports in Brazil of microcephaly were noticeably low, which indicated to analysts that it was being underreported. Then Zika arrived, and Brazilian reports of microcephaly spiked dramatically, causing some to believe that it was now being overreported due to sudden attentiveness on the health authorities' part. Since Zika became endemic in Brazil, more than 2,000 cases of CNS malformation have been recorded, and while the medical community took the situation seriously because of the health threat to newborns, it remained indecisive about the connection to Zika. However, a subset of Zika-related microcephaly cases created a solid argument for calling them "Zika-induced." Some babies exhibited fetal brain disruption sequence, a condition Dr. William Dobyns, a professor in the Departments of Pediatrics and Neurology at the University of Washington, described in contrast to average microcephaly:

> *In a fetus with microcephaly linked to a genetic cause, the brain grows more slowly so the skull grows more slowly. Although the overall head is small, the brain fits the skull. In contrast, if there is normal brain growth pushing the skull out and then at some point the brain is severely damaged and shrinks, the skull doesn't shrink. Soft tissue can shrink, but bones do not. In such cases, there is nothing to support the skull bones and they collapse over each other. This is not rare. It occurs in half of all infants with congenital Zika syndrome.*[13]

The occurrence of this condition means that Zika interrupted the development process, demonstrating that the virus has a direct effect on prenatal development.

Although the difference between "correlated" and "caused by" may not seem significant, the distinction matters. Just because two things seem connected does not mean they necessarily are, and researchers have to be sure that a disease causes a certain symptom before they tell the public, or they could cause needless panic. There was strong evidence, however, to suggest that Zika does, in fact, cause birth defects, and a report from the CDC encouraged the medical community to admit it for the sake of public health:

> *Moving from a hypothesis that Zika virus is linked to certain adverse outcomes to a statement that Zika virus is a cause of certain adverse outcomes allows for direct communications regarding risk, both in clinical care settings and in public health guidance, and an intensified focus on prevention efforts, such as the implementation of vector control, the identification of improved diagnostic methods, and the development of a Zika virus vaccine.*[14]

In order to get rid of Zika, a community effort had to be made to find both preventative measures and effective treatments for it. The only way to save newborns from Zika-related microcephaly is to keep their mothers from getting Zika, but the medical community could not do that if it did not become a united front against the disease. In April 2016, the CDC officially announced that Zika was a cause of microcephaly, and research to find out why began soon after.

Diagnosis

Because of the ways in which it is transmitted—by mosquito bite and by sexual contact—people only need to be tested for Zika in certain circumstances. The CDC released guidelines for who should be tested for Zika. "If you have symptoms of Zika or are a pregnant woman, with or without symptoms, Zika testing is recommended if: You live in or traveled to an area with Zika, [or] you had sex with a partner who lives in or traveled to an area with Zika,"[15] announced a CDC flyer from July 2016.

Zika mimics many other diseases, so diagnosing it simply by assessing symptoms is not recommended. Even if a patient has Zika-like symptoms, they may have dengue or chikungunya instead, both of which are transmitted by mosquitoes in most places where Zika is found. Therefore, blood or urine tests are required to determine what illness a patient has. If the patient has reported their symptoms or come in for testing one to two weeks after they were infected, Zika virus RNA is generally easy to find in a urine sample. After two weeks, however, doctors need to test a serum of blood for Zika antibodies. The virus's RNA stays in the body for only about two weeks, but antibodies are generally found for about twelve weeks after infection. Testing for other diseases such as dengue and chikungunya is done in relatively the same manner, so patients may be tested for them, too, so as to avoid misdiagnosis based on copycat symptoms.

Zika mimics so many other diseases that only a blood or urine test can determine what illness a patient has.

Test results generally return in two to four weeks, just long enough for most Zika symptom sufferers to feel better. The CDC reminds people to review their results whether or not they are feeling better, since experts have not yet determined how long someone is contagious for, so someone may be at risk of passing Zika on even if they no longer have symptoms.

Treatment

As of June 2017, no vaccine or medicine for Zika has become available. Because it was such a low-profile disease until the outbreak in Brazil, researchers did not believe it was worth the time or money it would take to create a treatment. Now, since Zika has been connected to both GBS and microcephaly, time and money are being diverted to study the disease and find a cure.

Although some would surely benefit in the short term from a medicine that would reverse Zika's effects after infection, researchers are more interested in keeping Zika from infecting people in the first place. "The need for a drug is less compelling than the need for a vaccine," said Dr. Anthony Fauci, director of the National Institute of Allergy and Infectious Diseases at the National Institutes of Health (NIH). "Since

Zika is an infection that in most people is usually gone within a few days, it may be tough to have a major impact with a drug as opposed to prevention, with a vaccine."[16] Vaccine development is currently underway at the NIH, and clinical trials are underway in the United States as well as some Central and South American countries. However, the vaccine will not be available to the public until testing is completed, which may not be until 2018—or later, if the tests do not prove that the vaccine works effectively.

The NIH

The NIH, also known as the National Institutes of Health, is part of the U.S. Department of Health and Human Services. It is located in Bethesda, Maryland, and is the primary agency of the U.S. government responsible for biomedical and health-related research. According to its website, the NIH "is made up of twenty-seven different components called Institutes and Centers. Each has its own specific research agenda, often focusing on particular diseases or body systems."[1] The National Institute of Allergy and Infectious Diseases (NIAID) is the part of the NIH leading the clinical trials of the Zika vaccine. The NIH can trace its roots to 1887, when it was created within the Marine Hospital Service, after Congress charged it with "examining passengers on arriving ships for clinical signs of infectious diseases, especially for the dreaded diseases cholera and yellow fever, in order to prevent epidemics."[2]

1. "History," National Institutes of Health, December 13, 2016. www.nih.gov/about-nih/who-we-are/history.

2. "History," National Institutes of Health.

Since there is presently no cure, doctors typically recommend treating Zika as if it were a cold. Bed rest, fluids, and fever and pain reducers such as acetaminophen are generally prescribed. Although some people respond better to aspirin and other nonsteroidal anti-inflammatory drugs (NSAIDs) when dealing with joint pain, they are not recommended until dengue fever is ruled out as the cause of symptoms because of the risk of NSAID-related bleeding. Steroid eyedrops may be prescribed for viral conjunctivitis, and anti-itching creams may be applied to the rash. These measures are meant to lessen the symptoms of Zika and make it easier to get through being sick, but they cannot make an individual better or spare them from the complications that could arise later. Because of this, avoiding infection is really the best way to deal with Zika.

CHAPTER THREE

TRANSMISSION AND PREVENTION

Zika is primarily a mosquito-borne virus like malaria, yellow fever, and West Nile virus, but unlike these related diseases, scientists have discovered that it can also be passed from one person to another through sexual contact. Additionally, since it is a blood-borne pathogen like the human immunodeficiency virus (HIV), it can be transmitted through blood transfusions. Worst of all, the virus has found a way to pass through the placenta, and its greatest danger lies in its ability to infect unborn children.

While it is difficult to keep mosquitoes from biting and even harder to protect a sexual partner when someone is not even aware they have been infected with Zika in the first place, there are simple, practical precautions and solutions that can be taken to help minimize exposure.

Through Mosquito Bites

Zika is carried by mosquitoes in the genus *Aedes*, primarily by the *Ae. aegypti* and *Ae. albopictus* species. Both species are originally from tropical and subtropical regions in Africa and Asia, but they are able to live in temperate zones as well, especially *Ae. albopictus*, which can hibernate through the winter in cold climates. Through trade, both *Ae. aegypti* and *Ae. albopictus* have spread to the United States. Their eggs end up in shipping containers; they hatch there,

Aedes aegypti, shown here, is one of two species that have been identified as carriers of the Zika virus.

and the mosquitoes are released once the containers reach their destinations.

Because they need blood to produce eggs, only female mosquitoes bite. Female mosquitoes can live up to 8 weeks, or about 56 days, and if they hibernate, they can live up to 6 months. This makes them very effective as transmitters for diseases such as Zika, as Dr. Rik Bleijs explained on his website:

> *The mosquitoes generally acquire the virus while feeding on the blood of an infected person. After virus incubation for eight to ten days, an infected mosquito is capable, during probing and blood feeding, of transmitting the virus for the rest of its life. There is no way to tell if a mosquito is carrying the Zika virus. Infected female mosquitoes may also transmit the virus to their offspring by transovarial (via the eggs) transmission, but the role of this in sustaining transmission of the virus to humans has not yet been defined.*
>
> *Infected humans are the main carriers and multipliers of the virus, and serving as a source of the virus for uninfected mosquitoes. The virus circulates in the blood of infected humans for several days, at approximately the same time that they have Zika fever.*[17]

This process began when a mosquito bit an infected primate in Africa and carried the disease to a human. Because apes are evolutionary cousins to humans, the immune systems tend to be similar, so Zika had very little trouble adapting quickly to its new environment: the human body. After that, the virus spread from human to human through mosquito bites and sexual activity.

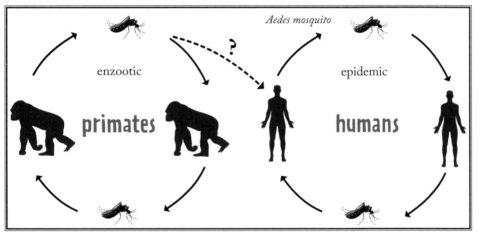

Zika was originally an enzootic disease, passed around from monkey to monkey through infected mosquitoes until an infected mosquito bit a human, as this information from the University of California, Davis, shows.

The simplest way to avoid mosquito bites is to stay away from areas where mosquitoes live and breed. Zika-spreading mosquitoes lay their eggs on "damp surfaces in areas likely to temporarily flood, such as tree holes and man-made containers,"[18] reported a fact sheet from Florida's Department of Agriculture and Consumer Services. Mosquito eggs are often found in buckets, old tires, flower pots—anything that will fill with water when it rains. "Most often, eggs will be placed at varying distances above the water line,"[19] the fact sheet continued. Then when the water rises, the eggs will be prompted to hatch. Health authorities suggest getting rid of standing water around the home or sealing it properly if it must be left outside. In Philadelphia, Pennsylvania, health authorities posted ads in 2017 with similar advice. The Philadelphia Department of Public Health fears travelers will become infected with the virus on vacation, come back to Philadelphia, and infect the *Ae. albopictus* mosquitoes that live there. About 200 cases of Zika were reported in Pennsylvania in 2015, but health officials successfully prevented the virus from being transferred to the native mosquitoes.

If travel to a place known to be home to *Ae. aegypti* mosquitoes is necessary, wear long sleeves and pants, stay inside and in air conditioning as much as possible, and use insect repellents that are registered by the Environmental Protection Agency (EPA). These have DEET, picaridin, IR3535, lemon eucalyptus oil, or para-menthane-diol as their active ingredient. Clothing and tents treated with permethrin, an insecticide that will repel and kill mosquitoes, are also available at most sporting goods stores.

Through Sexual Contact

The first-known case of sexually transmitted Zika was in the United States in 2008 when a tropical-disease researcher came home from Senegal and gave the disease to his wife. Since then, there have been 38 documented cases of sexually transmitted Zika in the United States and about 60 cases recorded worldwide. More than 10 countries have reported sex-related Zika infections, including England, which had its first sex-related case in November 2016.

Although it is not technically classified as a sexually transmitted disease (STD), Zika behaves quite a bit like other sexually transmitted viruses such as herpes, HPV, and HIV, which are each so effective because their main mode of transmission is through mucous membranes, which are some of the body's most vulnerable areas. NAM, a British nonprofit organization that focuses on spreading information and awareness about HIV and AIDS, defines mucous membranes as "the moist membranes lining body cavities that are not protected by skin: this includes the mouth and oesophagus, the nostrils, the eye sockets, and the rectum. Genital areas covered by mucous membranes include the vagina, the urethra, and the underside of the foreskin."[20] Because mucous membranes are essentially the last line of defense between the internal organs and the outside world, they are full of dendritic cells—cells specifically designed to transfer infectious particles to the lymph nodes through the bloodstream. In order to do their job, however, these cells must allow viruses into the body, and once there, they can begin to replicate while traveling from the entry site to the lymph nodes. Lymph nodes are full of white blood cells and are meant to filter out and destroy foreign elements in the blood, but some viruses, such as Zika, can establish themselves in the body too quickly for the white blood cells to prevent infection.

During sex, many of these mucous membranes come into contact with bodily fluids that may carry the Zika virus if one partner has been infected. Once infected, any bodily fluid can carry the virus; in addition to blood and urine, which are used in Zika diagnostic tests, semen, vaginal fluids, and saliva have also been proven to carry the disease. "Studies are underway to find out how long Zika stays in the semen and vaginal fluids of people who have Zika, and how long it can be passed to sex partners. Current research shows that Zika can remain in semen longer than in other body fluids, including vaginal fluids, urine, and blood,"[21] said the CDC. According to some studies, Zika can be found for up to 21 days in urine and saliva, but it can be found for as long as 93 days in semen, making sexually active males a bigger risk for infection than their female counterparts. What scientists are finding by the end of these time periods are molecular traces of the virus, which may or may not be infectious. However, the fact that they are there suggests that an active, possibly infectious version of the virus was there at some point. Researchers simply do not know when these particles become inactive, which makes it difficult to tell when the transmission risk is over.

A common question about Zika that is most often associated with sexual transmission is, "Can someone with no symptoms infect someone else?" The answer is yes. Eighty percent of all people who are infected with Zika show no symptoms at all, but the virus is still in their systems, making them equally as infectious as someone with a fever and a rash. Because of this, the CDC recommends that everyone should employ basic safe sex methods to prevent the spread of Zika between sexual partners. Condoms, whether male or female, should be used from start to finish during any sexual encounter, and dental dams (small latex or polyurethane sheets) should be used during oral sex specifically. This

Safe sex methods should be used to prevent the spread of Zika between sexual partners.

is especially crucial for pregnant women, since recent studies have shown that sexually transmitted Zika is equally as likely to interfere with fetus development as mosquito-transmitted Zika. It is also important to remember that these precautions apply to everyone, not just heterosexual men. "Public health experts now know that Zika can be passed in bodily fluids between one man and another, between a man and a woman, and from a woman to a man—and though no case has been made public, they assume it can be transmitted between female partners as well,"[22] pointed out global health journalist Maryn McKenna in *National Geographic*. This means that everyone, regardless of sexuality or gender, should practice safe sex to stop the spread of Zika as well as other STDs.

Control and Prevention

The CDC is a federal agency under the Department of Health and Human Services. It is headquartered in Atlanta, Georgia. Its goal is to "protect America from health, safety, and security threats, both foreign and in the US ... [The] CDC conducts critical science and provides health information to the public that protects our nation against expensive and dangerous health threats, and responds when these arise."[1]

It opened its doors in 1946 as the Communicable Disease Center. Tasked with preventing malaria from spreading across the United States, its first mission was to wage war on mosquitoes. It is taking on that task again with the new threat of Zika looming on the horizon.

1. "Mission, Role and Pledge," Centers for Disease Control and Prevention, April 14, 2016. www.cdc.gov/about/organization/mission.htm.

From Mother to Child

After Zika became connected with microcephaly, scientists began studying how the disease is transmitted to the fetus, and for a while, they were puzzled. Flaviviruses such as Zika are rarely passed from mother to child because of the placenta, an organ that grows during pregnancy and connects the fetus to the uterine wall. The placenta creates a barrier between the fetus and its mother and keeps their circulatory systems separate, which makes it difficult for some diseases to infect both individuals. It was discovered, however, that Zika has the special ability to hide inside host cells and cross the placental barrier undetected.

Researchers at the Emory University School of Medicine discovered Zika's trick. To monitor Zika's effects on the placenta, placental cells were grown in the lab from samples taken from five different women

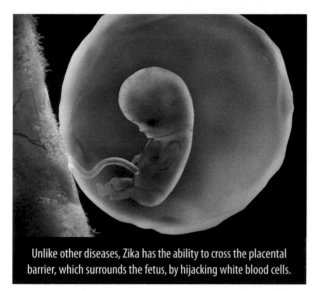

Unlike other diseases, Zika has the ability to cross the placental barrier, which surrounds the fetus, by hijacking white blood cells.

and were then infected with a Zika strain from Puerto Rico. Soon after, researchers observed the production of Hofbauer cells, a type of white blood cell that would have had access to fetal blood vessels if the lab-grown placenta had been connected to a fetus. These cells "eat" foreign particles, but when they eat Zika, Zika hijacks them, meaning that it would be able to enter the fetus's bloodstream wearing a Hofbauer disguise. From there, it could infect fetal brain tissue and this, scientists believe, is how microcephaly is caused. Each sample reacted differently, however, meaning that not all women who carry the Zika virus will necessarily infect their unborn child if they become pregnant or are pregnant when they contract Zika.

The CDC's guidelines for having a safe pregnancy during the Zika epidemic encourage women to avoid getting pregnant for eight weeks after they may have been exposed to the disease. In places where Zika is not locally transmitted, this means eight weeks after a woman or her partner has traveled to an infected area; in places where Zika is widespread, this means eight weeks after a positive Zika test. During pregnancy, women are advised to reduce their possible exposure to Zika as much as possible up until the end of the first trimester, when fetuses are most vulnerable to Zika-related brain damage. Men, on the other hand, are being told to wait six months before attempting to conceive, since infectious Zika may be transmittable through semen for more than 90 days.

At first, some people worried that Zika could be transmitted from mother to child during breastfeeding, but there have been no instances of babies being infected in that way. Even in countries with widespread local transmission of Zika, infants who were born without microcephaly have shown no signs of acquiring neurological issues if they were infected after birth. Mothers are told to continue breastfeeding their infants as they would normally.

Through Blood Transfusion

Since the Zika virus is mainly transmitted by blood, the possibility that it could be passed from person to person through blood transfusion has been very real since the beginning. In spite of testing and irradiation—the process of exposing donated blood to gamma radiation—diseased blood still sometimes makes its way into hospital rooms and operating rooms, causing clusters of infection in certain areas. While there have been no recorded instances of such a thing happening with the Zika virus in the United States, Brazil has reported two confirmed cases of Zika infection via blood transfusion.

These two cases happened in January 2016. A presymptomatic Zika patient donated blood on January 16, not knowing they had been infected. Two units of their blood were collected, irradiated, and transfused into two different patients—a 54-year-old woman and a 14-year-old girl—on January 19. Two days later, on January 21, the donor called the blood bank to report a rash, eye pain, and joint pain in their knees that had started on January 18. These symptoms suggested Zika, and blood tests from the donor confirmed Zika infection

14 days later. Both the older woman and young girl who had received the donor's blood were also tested, and they were both positive for Zika as well. Although neither ever displayed symptoms, doctors confirmed that they had contracted the same strain as their donor, indicating that blood transfusion was the cause of their infection.

Blood banks and hospitals try their hardest to keep infected blood out of the supply of donated units. Thorough screening happens through questionnaires given to donors before they donate and laboratory testing. Currently, tests for Chagas disease, hepatitis B and C, HIV, human T-lymphotropic virus, syphilis, and West Nile virus are done on every unit of blood that goes through the American Red Cross. However, these tests are very specific and do not indicate if any other disease is present in a sample. Irradiation is used to kill other infectious particles that may go undetected, but it is not 100 percent effective. Recently, the CDC has condoned the use of non-FDA-licensed tests for Zika on donated units of blood and has advised health authorities to dispose of blood that returns positive for the virus.

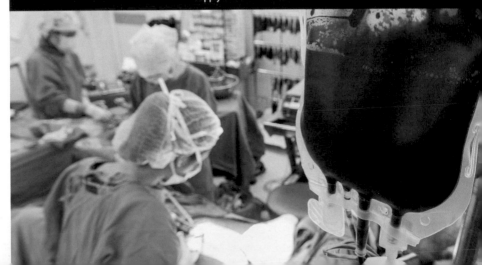

Although it is possible for Zika to be passed from person to person through blood transfusion, blood banks and hospitals are using a combination of irradiation and testing to try to keep infected blood out of the supply of donated units.

Blood Donor Eligibility

The American Red Cross conforms to strict standards in order to protect the people who receive blood donations from disease. People with histories of intravenous drug use, positive HIV tests, or certain STDs are not allowed to give blood, and people who have been infected with Zika have now been added to that list.

Some other criteria, however, are rather surprising. People may not give blood if, in the previous 12 months, they have been pierced with a reusable piercing gun or any reusable instrument or have been tattooed at all. Additionally, men who have had sex with other men (MSM) may not give blood for 12 months after their sexual encounter. This requirement was changed in December 2015; MSM used to not be allowed to donate blood at any time because of their higher risk for HIV/AIDS, but many found that to be discriminatory. According to the Red Cross, "This policy change aligns the MSM donor deferral period with those for other activities that may pose a similar risk of transfusion-transmissible infections."[1] In other words, there was no reason to ban people for life when the risk of transmitting infection was the same as for diseases that only required a one-year waiting period.

1. "Eligibility Criteria: Alphabetical," American Red Cross. www.redcrossblood.org/donating-blood/eligibility-requirements/eligibility-criteria-alphabetical-listing.

Further Precautions

The CDC recommends using reasonable caution when living with or helping someone who has contracted Zika. The most important step is protecting oneself from an infected person's bodily fluids, which is sometimes easier said than done when dealing with a sick person. In contrast to many other illnesses, Zika is not known for causing expulsions of body fluid, but even everyday coughing, sneezing, and accidental cuts can bring an uninfected person into contact with infected saliva and blood. Although Zika has not been found to be transmittable through saliva, the best thing to do is simply wash one's hands after providing care to a Zika patient and use household disinfectants to clean the patient's environment daily, just to be safe. All in all, Zika is much more difficult to transmit in close quarters than a cold or the flu, but precautions are not unnecessary, especially if the caregiver is pregnant or plans on becoming pregnant in the near future.

When dealing with Zika patients, simple precautions such as washing hands as well as keeping the environment clean and disinfected can help stop its spread.

The CDC has also provided suggestions for creating a Zika prevention kit for those who live in places where Zika is spreading locally. The kit should include bed netting if a bedroom is not mosquito-proof; standing water treatment tablets to kill mosquito larvae in standing water around the home; bug repellant to prevent mosquitoes from biting; and permethrin spray for extra protection on clothing when going outside. Condoms are also recommended for people who are sexually active. Having these things on hand during a local Zika outbreak can greatly reduce the possibility of infection if used correctly and together.

Where Is Zika Now?

In all of South America, Central America, and the Caribbean islands, only Chile and Uruguay have not reported any local transmissions of Zika as of January 2017. These two countries have each reported at least one confirmed case of Zika, but in each case, it was due to someone who had traveled to another country and brought the infection back with them. When the virus first burst into the public eye at the end of 2015, Dr. Anthony Fauci of the NIH discussed a couple of reasons why it was spreading so far so quickly:

> *Well, one of the reasons that we see spread like this ... is that, up until now, South America and the Caribbean has been what we call immunologically naive to Zika virus. They have never had Zika virus in the Western Hemisphere or in the Americas.*
>
> *And so when a new infection like this comes in, there's no background immunity in the population that would blunt the outbreak that we're seeing now, whereas something like dengue infection has been prevalent in South America, particularly in Brazil, for several years now. So there's that background immunity to it. No such immunity with Zika.*
>
> *It's perfectly new to them, which makes it much, much easier to explode in the population. That, together with the fact that they're loaded with mosquitoes, who are the vectors of this particular virus infection. The Aedes aegypti mosquitoes are all over South America and Brazil, and that's the perfect vector to spread this infection.*[23]

Despite the widespread infection risk in South and Central America, the CDC has kept the travel warning for these countries at Level 2, suggesting enhanced caution when visiting but not advising avoidance unless the traveler is a pregnant woman. This has caused some outcry, since even cautious travel to infected areas can bring the virus home and spread it to local mosquitoes. House representatives even wrote a letter to President Barack Obama asking him to raise the warning to Level 3, halting all nonessential travel, but nothing came of it.

Since then, the United States has experienced its first locally transmitted Zika cases. In Miami-Dade County, Florida, and Brownsville, Texas, mosquitoes have begun to transmit Zika among residents. This is believed to be for two reasons: First, they are some of the southernmost states, making them the closest to infected areas in Mexico and the Caribbean; and second, their climates are highly conducive to mosquito breeding, making the overall possible number of infected mosquitoes higher. Both *Ae. aegypti* and *Ae. albopictus* live much farther north than Florida and Texas as well, which is reason for caution everywhere in the country. So far, there have been no reports of local transmission from Canada, but even that could change.

The cases of Zika reported in Texas and Florida prompted the Florida Department of Health to set up a temporary clinic in the Miami Beach Police Department, offering free Zika testing.

In Africa, only the tiny island nation of Cape Verde has recorded local transmission of Zika during the recent epidemic. Although doctors think previous strains of Zika may still be circulating on the mainland, they are distantly related to the strain that is currently plowing through the Americas and are unlikely to have the same health risks. Also, as Fauci said, Africans have a baseline immunity to Zika because it has been in the area for so long. The same goes for most of Southeast Asia. The strain that appeared in Brazil is more closely related to the Asian strain of the virus than the African one, but it has evolved its health complications as it spread. In these areas, Zika is most likely not reported anymore because even on the rare occasion that someone shows symptoms, they are most likely treated as the symptoms of a cold. In Asia and the Pacific Islands, only American Samoa, Fiji, Kosrae (part of the Federated States of Micronesia), the Marshall Islands, New Caledonia, Palau, Papua New Guinea, Samoa, Singapore, and Tonga have reported what they believe to be the new strain of Zika from Brazil. Because of the spread of the new strain, testing for Zika is becoming more common all over the world, so it is being found more often and in more places. Because people from uninfected countries continue to travel to infected areas, the risk of transmission becoming local in previously unaffected places is very high. The most people can do is try to protect themselves, and by doing so, protect others from catching the disease.

CHAPTER FOUR

THE SOCIAL REALITIES OF ZIKA

No one wants to contract Zika or cope with the impact it can have on their lives. Unfortunately, thousands have already been affected by the disease's aftermath, and there is no telling how many more will be infected before it is finally brought under control.

Although the media's focus has been on the babies born to women who contracted the virus, Zika does not discriminate. Its victims include not only infants with microcephaly, but also their mothers, who must face the daily struggle of raising a child with physical, developmental, and cognitive disabilities. It drives a wedge between couples, dividing husbands from wives who hope to conceive, and it ostracizes victims of the disease from family and friends who wonder if they are still contagious. The disease is mild and the chances of contracting it in the United States are small, especially if the proper precautions are taken, but the media's focus on it has made many people fearful and suspicious.

Zika's impact on the economy is far-reaching as well. With many tropical vacation spots identified as vectors for the virus, the influx of tourist dollars threatens to dry up as travel to these destinations falls off.

More Than a Mild Inconvenience

For some Zika sufferers, the illness tends not to leave a lasting impression. Such was the case for

Kevin McGinnis, a man who travels to Brazil every year to visit his wife's family. While returning to the United States after a trip in the summer of 2015, McGinnis began feeling strange; his back hurt, and he felt generally out of sorts. A few days later, his wife pointed out the red bumps appearing on his arms as they were driving, and when they got home, he discovered that they had covered his entire torso. A trip to an urgent care clinic confirmed Zika, which McGinnis's wife had only recently heard about from her family in Brazil. McGinnis's case, however, was mild, as expected, and he recovered within a week. "It was, for me, a non-event," he told local news. "Seriously, the cold I have now is worse than that!"[24]

In other cases, though, Zika can throw off the balance of someone's life. Nick Brown, a reporter for the news outlet Reuters, accepted a yearlong post in Puerto Rico four months before Zika arrived on the island. Six months later, he found himself sick, complaining of fever, a skin rash, joint and eye pain, and even pain and redness in what he described as an "exclusively male region"[25] for two weeks. A week after he began to feel better, however, his symptoms came back—plus headaches and severe fatigue. When he returned home for a visit, he went to his doctor. After describing his symptoms, his doctor ordered a blood test, and Brown was diagnosed with Zika. Although his symptoms had gone away by that time, his infection threw a cloud over his life back home:

> Some friends in Puerto Rico teased me when they learned I had Zika. Many of them had experienced chikungunya or dengue, and had stories about months of muscle pain or weeks in bed. Friends from the states, on the other hand, showed grave concern, offering thoughts, prayers and condolences. Some kept their distance for weeks. A few questioned whether it was safe for me to be around babies ...

As the weeks passed, it became clear that Julie [my wife] and I were also a little rattled—and not fully on the same page. She canceled a planned long weekend visit to Puerto Rico. She wanted to minimize her exposure to Zika and arranged instead for us to meet in Florida.

This disappointed me. I had hoped to show her my new favorite places on the island. I clung stubbornly to the view that Zika fears were largely overblown. She reminded me that, given the unknowns about Zika's impact on pregnancy, I was in no position to call the shots.

"Try to see it from a woman's perspective," she said.[26]

Not only did Brown's friends back away, but his relationship with his wife became strained. The possibility of infecting her through sexual intercourse, as well as confusing mixed messages from doctors about how long they should wait to have a child, put emotional distance between them and made their future seem very far away. Brown's experience and his wife's concern are surely common, suggesting an emotional toll on top of the physical toll that comes with Zika. While putting off having a child may seem like an easy thing to do, in reality it is often not, especially when birth control is hard to come by.

Zika's impact on the lives of its victims is felt on many levels and can negatively affect relationships with friends and family.

The Birth Control Struggle

With both Planned Parenthood and health insurance in jeopardy because of the political climate following the 2016 U.S. presidential election, many American women fear that it may become harder to acquire birth control in the future. Although condoms can be bought in drug stores and birth control pills can be picked up from a pharmacy with a prescription, they are considered nonessential items and are often overpriced, prohibiting people who would otherwise use them from getting ahold of them. Planned Parenthood, a nonprofit organization that provides reproductive health services, often offers condoms for free and is a resource for affordable birth control, but there is often talk in Congress about defunding it, and its future financial status is uncertain. A lack of funds will affect the care the organization can offer. Health insurance, too, has become more expensive and more difficult to get, moving contraception even farther from the people who need it. Because of this, the CDC's call for more thorough use of birth control to prevent Zika from spreading may be ignored.

"There is a substantial overlap between the areas at greatest risk for Zika virus spread and those populations with the poorest access to quality reproductive health services," said Jeffrey Klausner, a professor of medicine and public health at UCLA. "Those are the areas and states in the Southeastern U.S. that border the Gulf of Mexico."[27] If an area does not have access to birth control, the odds of Zika being sexually transmitted go up dramatically, and the odds of unwanted pregnancy in women who may have been infected with Zika also go up, potentially leading to more babies born with microcephaly. Many lawmakers, however, have made it clear that they do not approve of birth control, even in extreme circumstances such as the Zika epidemic. In 2016, a funding bill aimed at providing aid against Zika had "an explicit provision that none of the $1.1 billion it included could be put toward Planned Parenthood, and provided no other money for contraception,"[28] Julie Beck reported in *The Atlantic*. This bill was rejected by the Senate, primarily because the lack of concern it showed for birth control's important role in managing Zika's spread could be damaging in the long run. After the provision was removed, the bill was passed.

In South and Central America, the conversation about contraception has turned Zika into a women's rights issue. The Global Fund for Women had this to say about the Zika outbreak:

With both health insurance and reproductive rights under fire, the odds of unwanted pregnancy in women who may have been infected with Zika are likely to go up.

Recommendations by government officials in Brazil, Colombia, Ecuador, and El Salvador for women to "avoid getting pregnant" only exposes the stark reality for many women and girls in Latin America, especially in rural areas. Most have minimal access to sexual and reproductive health and rights or education ... There are high levels of misinformation—for instance, most women and girls are not educated about contraception or family planning due to strong conservative rhetoric.[29]

Most Latin American countries are predominately Catholic, meaning that they tend to strongly disapprove of birth control and abortion. In some countries, such as El Salvador, the Dominican Republic, and Nicaragua, abortion has been outlawed entirely. Because of this, many Latin American women are essentially forced into pregnancies they may not want. With Zika on the loose, many women do not wish to risk having a miscarriage or to risk the health of an unborn child, but using birth control or having an abortion to spare themselves and their child from suffering is not seen as an option. Organizations such as the Global Fund for Women have begun to fight on behalf of these women, trying to make information about reproductive rights more widely available and attempting to give them the freedom to do what they wish with their own bodies.

Mothers of Angels

União de Mães de Anjos, or the Union of Mothers of Angels—UMA for short—is a community based in Recife, Brazil, for mothers of children who have been born with microcephaly because of Zika. On Facebook, they share parenting advice, pictures, and updates on public health meetings, as well as support and encouragement for the increasing number of new mothers of babies with microcephaly. Offline, however, they and their children face discrimination despite their ever-growing numbers. Katherine Jinyi Li, a freelance journalist in Brazil, went to meet with these mothers. In her article for the *Seattle Globalist*, she wrote,

> But the stories the mothers told me of the treatment their babies received on a daily basis because of their condition appalled me. Stories of people staring and asking intrusive health questions on the streets, pulling their own children away for fear of contagion, and refusing the mothers entry onto public buses because of their "demon babies" were common.

> UMA members regularly gather to walk the city streets with their babies wrapped in cotton

carrier slings, holding banners that read "Micro-cephaly is not the end" and "Our children don't need your pity, they need your respect."[30]

In Recife, Brazil, mothers of children with Zika-induced microcephaly meet regularly to share parenting advice and to support and encourage each other.

Some of these mothers are looking for government help and feel entitled to it, given that many health authorities missed diagnosing their children with microcephaly before the connection to Zika was drawn. Mostly, they are asking for developmental support such as early intervention services so their children can have a good chance at maximizing their potential. In the end, their main motivation is their love for their babies, whom they do not wish to see be forgotten or left behind because of their disabilities.

Bad for Business

One of the reasons for the American government's hesitation to ban all travel to Zika-infected areas is the impact that action would have on the tourist industries in those countries. Tourist industries are made up of the service industries that cater to tourism. Transportation such as airlines and taxi services, accommodations such as hotels and resorts, and entertainment venues all contribute to a country's GDP, or gross domestic product, which is the total amount of money the country makes in a year. In countries such as Aruba and the British Virgin Islands, tourism makes up a large amount of the nations' yearly income, and a good portion of that comes from America, since the United States is the Caribbean's primary market. If the United States decided its people could no longer go to these places on vacation, their economies would crumble.

The tourism industry in countries such as Aruba (shown here) and the British Virgin Islands would collapse if travel from the United States to those high-risk locations was restricted.

Even for countries that rely less on the money of American tourists, Zika has cost them a lot. Puerto Rico, for example, takes in only about 7 percent of its GDP through its tourist industries, but it has felt the impact of the CDC's travel warnings in a big way. Ingrid I. Rivera Rocafort, executive director of the Puerto Rico Tourism Company, described to a reporter at the *Washington Post* how hotel registrations went down 5 percent after the CDC issued its first warnings for pregnant women at the beginning of 2016. "Forty-one thousand room nights were canceled going forward up to two years. That's a loss of $28 million for 2016 through the end of 2017 and the beginning of 2018,"[31] she explained.

According to a report issued in April 2017 by the United Nations Development Programme (UNDP) and the International Federation of Red Cross and Red Crescent Societies (IFRC), Zika cost Latin America and the Caribbean an estimated $7–18 billion between 2015 and 2017. This includes not just economic costs, but social costs as well. Poorer countries suffer more from the consequences of Zika than wealthier ones, partially because good health care is not as readily available in those areas, especially to the poorest members of the population. The Caribbean was hit harder than South America, particularly Haiti and Belize. According to Jessica Faieta, the UN assistant secretary-general and UNDP director for Latin America and the Caribbean, "Aside from tangible losses to GDP and to economies heavily dependent on tourism, and the stresses on health care systems, the long-term consequences of the Zika virus can undermine decades of social development, hard-earned health gains and slow down progress towards the Sustainable Development Goals."[32] One financial side effect is the loss of income for women who must stay home and care for their developmentally disabled children; this loss, according to the report, is expected to reach as high as $5 billion in the Caribbean.

Some people were concerned the United States might suffer a similar loss of tourism, although the consequences would not be nearly as severe. A $24 billion tourism spot, Miami contributes the third most sales tax to the state of Florida, and some business owners worried that the industry would lose money because of Zika. Fortunately for the state, the summer of 2016 did not bring a decline in Florida tourism despite the first local Zika transmissions there; in fact, it broke records for how many people visited the state. This increase, however, was mostly likely due to an aggressive advertising campaign, which may or may not have been misleading about the risk of Zika infection.

Too Seriously or Not Seriously Enough

Although many Americans are well-informed about the Zika virus and its threats, recent polls suggest that just as many are not. In a survey conducted by the Harvard Opinion Research Program at Harvard's T.H. Chan School of Public Health in Boston, Massachusetts, researchers found that 20 percent of Americans were not aware that Zika could be transmitted from mother to child during pregnancy, and one out of four people did not know about the connection between Zika and microcephaly. About 40 percent did not realize that Zika can be sexually transmitted. One out of five people believe that a vaccine for Zika exists, even though there is no such vaccine and no media outlet has ever reported the existence of one, and 25 percent of people thought that a person with Zika would be "very likely" to show symptoms. The fact that so many do not know how Zika is transmitted besides mosquito bites or how Zika can affect people is concerning for public health.

While many Americans are well-informed about the Zika virus and its threats, recent polls suggest that almost as many are not.

"Some of those [misconceptions] could prevent people at risk from taking steps to protect their pregnancies," said Gillian SteelFisher, deputy director of the Harvard Opinion Research Program. "And, then there's the reverse problem, which is there are some misconceptions that could cause people to take unnecessary or inappropriate precautions."[33] Another poll, conducted by CNN and ORC International, indicated that this tends to be true. Of those who responded to the poll, 77 percent said they were "not too worried" or "not worried at all" about Zika, while 5 percent reported being "very worried" about it. According to this survey, that means only 18 percent of Americans are "somewhat worried," which is a reasonable level of worry for the current situation. For Americans, Zika does not warrant extreme caution, but it also does not deserve to be ignored. Precautions should be taken, but there is no reason to panic. In spite of this, however, these polls suggest that the media is not doing its job of correctly informing the population about Zika.

Actions Americans Have Taken to Avoid Contracting Zika

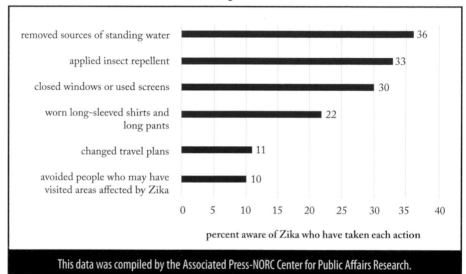

This data was compiled by the Associated Press-NORC Center for Public Affairs Research.

Media Coverage

News and media outlets have always tended to inflate the truth; ratings are important, after all, and marketing teams found out a long time ago that reporting the simple facts does not intrigue the average viewer or reader. Even when the truth is not inflated, it is presented in a sensationalized way. Shocking statistics are often presented first, then the reality of those statistics is explained; this means someone who only reads the beginning of an article or catches the first few minutes of a news broadcast may not get the full picture. Because of this, the public receives a distorted version of the truth, and that has become apparent in Zika's case. Paul Senatori from MediaQuant, a media statistics company, pointed out the problem with the kind of coverage Zika has had:

> *The perceived view—gained through media "reports"—that Zika cannot be "contained" is the key driver in how people respond to the disease. For example, while influenza may affect and kill millions every year, the perception that it can be contained, i.e., via flu shots, vaccinations, viral medicines, rest, fluids, etc. makes it a relatively minor disease, at least from a media perspective. Versus Zika, which has horrendous health implications, but is not nearly as prevalent in the human population.*
>
> *But Zika's lack of "containment" drives media coverage. In some ways it's more about the size of the threat than the* risk *of the threat that piques media interest.*[34]

What Zika media coverage seems to lack is solid facts and statistics. News outlets talk about how widespread Zika is but rarely bring up how unlikely an individual is to get infected; in the United States, about 5,500 people have contracted Zika both at home and abroad, but that is only 0.000016 percent of the population. Even in the places in Brazil with the highest incidence rates of Zika, only about 0.7 percent of the population has been infected. These statistics, however, are not generally shared with the public because they do not communicate the necessary scale of the disease.

What is interesting about the media coverage of Zika is that it seems to have had the opposite effect on many people than analysts would expect. In times of epidemic, sensationalized news tends to drive panic,

Instead of focusing on the facts, which could help individuals protect themselves from Zika and help break the cycle of infection, the media has instead sensationalized and distorted the disease's reputation.

and while there is certainly some of that surrounding Zika, a large number of people have decided not to worry about it at all. However, this is almost unsurprising. Americans have gotten worked up over global epidemics before—SARS, bird flu, swine flu, and Ebola have all had their time in the spotlight, being hailed as signs of the apocalypse—but very little has come of any of them, even if they have eventually made their way to the United States. To many, being worried about Zika may seem useless, and to a certain extent, it might be. Over the past 25 years, U.S. health authorities have done a relatively good job of keeping the public healthy. This does not, however, give the American people the right to ignore problems occurring in other countries or to endanger others by being careless.

Swine Flu Panic

H1N1, better known as swine flu, is a strain of influenza that originated in pigs. In 2009, a young boy in Mexico named Edgar became the first person to have ever been infected with it, and over the next few weeks, people began to panic. Despite being a relatively average flu, swine flu was found in many different places around the globe at roughly the same time, making it an anomaly for sure. The media took the story and ran with it, overhyping the possibility of the disease's mutation and making people think it could become the plague to end all plagues. It was deemed a pandemic, and over the course of a year, it may have killed over 200,000 people. While the death toll was higher than the average flu, which kills tens of thousands of people each year, the world did not end. A vaccine was created, and most people who were infected recovered.

Conspiracy Theories

Since there is so little information for authorities to give to the public about Zika and since the media insists on giving out even less information than there is available, the disease remains surrounded by mystery. This makes it the perfect target for conspiracy theories, most suggesting that the Zika infection was caused for the benefit of one corporation or another. While the variations are seemingly endless, there are a few common theories that have made their way into the public consciousness.

The first and most widely believed conspiracy theory about Zika is that genetically modified mosquitoes caused the disease in some way. In 2012, the British company Oxitec began introducing genetically modified male mosquitoes into the Brazilian mosquito population. These male mosquitoes were modified to pass on lethal genes to their offspring to fight the spread of dengue fever. In 2016, an Internet user jumped to the conclusion that these mosquitoes were somehow responsible for Zika. Despite having no evidence to back it up, this theory became an alarmingly false part of the public's understanding about Zika, with almost a third of Americans believing it to be true. The truth is that there is nothing about the genetically modified mosquitoes in South America that would affect humans. Their only purpose is to decrease the mosquito population by spreading bad genes to members of their own species.

Other conspiracy theories suggest that Zika is not the cause of the recent increase in microcephaly cases. Both pesticides and vaccines have been blamed instead, each for different reasons. The pesticide pyriproxyfen is used to prevent mosquito eggs from hatching by altering their hormones, and it is this interference with the species' young that had people drawing connections to microcephaly. Humans, however, have no hatching hormones to be altered, and their bodies are also very bad at absorbing pyriproxyfen, which is what makes it a good pesticide. Vaccines, too, had fingers pointed at them, this time by anti-vaxxers, a community of people who misguidedly believe vaccines can cause developmental issues. These claims were debunked almost as soon as they arose.

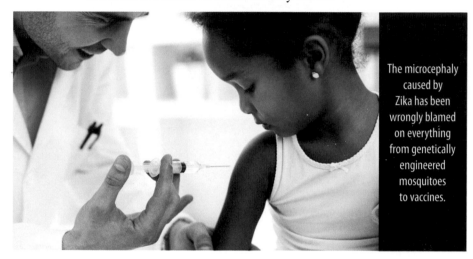

The microcephaly caused by Zika has been wrongly blamed on everything from genetically engineered mosquitoes to vaccines.

Although conspiracy theories can be interesting to speculate about, they can be harmful if the public believes them instead of actual scientific fact. Drawing attention away from Zika to blame genetic modification, pesticides, or vaccines diminishes its threat, which does not help people make informed decisions about their health and safety. Instead of trying to find a scapegoat for the effects of Zika, time and energy should be focused on finding ways to keep the disease from hurting more people in the future.

CHAPTER FIVE

LOOKING TO THE FUTURE

The WHO declared the global Zika crisis over in late 2016, but people are still concerned that it could make a comeback, especially when travelers take vacations to Zika-affected areas. Additionally, some are still feeling its effects. For instance, since January 2016, 16 babies have been diagnosed with Zika-related birth defects in New York City. For this reason, many United States cities, including New York and Philadelphia, are launching public awareness campaigns to educate Americans about the dangers of Zika.

Because it is imperative for Zika to be stopped in its tracks as soon as possible, a worldwide effort is underway to find answers. While researchers in the United States try to crack Zika's genetic code in order to create a vaccine, synthetic biology companies look for ways to eradicate the species of mosquitoes that carry the virus. Another promising line of research being conducted in Australia involves introducing bacteria into the insects' digestive tracts, which will render them incapable of passing on the Zika virus.

In the meantime, researchers have once again turned to rhesus monkeys in order to study natural immunity, and while organizations such as the WHO are hesitant to make sweeping statements, early experiments show that Zika does give a certain amount of immunity against re-infection. While this does not help people avoid infection, at least this information offers a glimmer of hope that those who have already had the disease will not have to go through it again.

What Will Happen if People Do Nothing?

Fragmented American politics are causing a fragmented response to Zika across the country and around the world, leaving many people at risk. The United States has been slow to provide public health and research funding and has debated whether or not to raise the CDC warning level, both of which are crucial steps to containing Zika's threat. Meanwhile, more people are being infected every day, raising both the financial and human cost of the virus.

Although President Obama signed a bill in September 2016, allocating $1.1 billion for addressing the Zika epidemic, the bill he signed had been contended in Congress for at least six months before reaching his desk. First called for by the president in February 2016, the bill was meant to fund the NIH and the CDC's research into a vaccine as well as give local health departments more resources to spread awareness about the disease. However, the bill was defeated in the Senate until Republicans and Democrats were forced to compromise because a government shutdown deadline was approaching. Democrats in the House of Representatives felt they could not sign off on a budget plan that ignored the importance of birth control in containing Zika, and eventually, Republicans who were pushing for funds to be prevented from going to Planned Parenthood gave up in the interest of moving forward.

Despite this, many counties are still underfunded. Local health departments do not have the budget to properly warn and educate the communities they serve about Zika. In this way, a lack of funding means a lack of awareness, which in turn, means unnecessary infections and a higher chance that someone may experience serious complications. The money from the government bill has not yet trickled down to the local level.

While some counties have been able to extend services such as free testing to their residents, many local health departments do not have the budget to warn and educate the communities they serve about the dangers of Zika.

Stopgap measures such as the Zika bill may also not be enough to fund the future in Latin America if Zika is not contained. As a major part of the global community and economy, the United States has taken on the responsibility of helping less wealthy countries in times of need. In an article for *Global Health and Diplomacy*, Dr. Kate Tulenko outlined some of the financial needs of Latin America during the Zika epidemic and how the United States is likely to spend its Zika budget:

> *The WHO estimates it needs $56 million to implement its Strategic Response Framework and Joint Operations Plan for Zika. The World Bank estimates Brazil alone will need $310 million for an effective response. The CDC has committed $25 million to Zika response in Puerto Rico and has asked Congress for $225 million more as part of President Obama's request for $1.8 billion in*

emergency funding. In all, Obama's request pack-
age includes $828 million for the CDC, but most
of that would go toward domestic response, with
little devoted to Latin America ...

But these estimates pale in comparison with the
costs we may incur after the epidemic.[35]

Tulenko estimated that the cost of waiting so long
to respond to Latin America's needs could be over
$5 billion, and the cost of waiting longer could double
or triple that number. These estimates are reached by
calculating the cost of medical and supportive care
that individuals with microcephaly will need over the
course of their lifetimes, and Tulenko suggested that
prolonging research and crippling local health departments would only make the cost higher.

The problem with Zika is that it has lingering
effects and causes a different kind of human cost than
the world has seen in a long time. Unlike SARS, bird
flu, or swine flu before it, Zika rarely ever kills people, but instead, it causes suffering, both physical and
emotional. Instead of leaving those who survive it to
move on and lead healthy lives, it may paralyze people, scare people out of having families, and damage
the brains of babies. If people continue to do nothing—to fail to support research and awareness efforts
and reduce the number of people infected—Zika
will continue to make life harder, and that is not fair
to anyone.

Minimizing Mosquitoes

In February 2016, the Maryland-based synthetic
biology company Intrexon Corporation announced
its development of genetically modified mosquitoes
that would help lower the mosquito population in
Zika-affected areas. Oxitec, Intrexon's British sub-
sidiary, had been testing the mosquitoes in Brazil for

WHO, Who?

The World Health Organization, or WHO, is an agency of the United Nations (UN). It was established on April 7, 1948, and is headquartered in Geneva, Switzerland. It is governed by the World Health Assembly, whose primary concern is international public health. Since its creation, it has played a leading role in the eradication of smallpox. Among its current priorities are "[increasing and sustaining] access to prevention, treatment and care for HIV, tuberculosis, malaria and neglected tropical diseases and to reduce vaccine-preventable diseases," and "leading and coordinating the health response in support of countries, undertaking risk assessments, identifying priorities and setting strategies, providing critical technical guidance, supplies and financial resources as well as monitoring the health situation."[1]

1. "What We Do," World Health Organization. www.who.int/about/what-we-do/en/.

years—leading some to falsely believe that they were the cause of the Zika outbreak there—but the sudden urgency for a solution to the mosquito problem in Latin America became an opportunity for Intrexon to have its work funded by Brazilian authorities.

Oxitec's mosquitoes are all male, and they are modified to produce offspring that will die before reaching adulthood and reproducing. Tests in Brazil and the Cayman Islands proved that this can effectively decrease the *Ae. aegypti* population by up to 90 percent. In March 2016, the U.S. Food and Drug Administration (FDA) approved the mosquitoes for trials in Florida, saying that they posed no risk to the environment. Florida residents were not too keen on the idea, however, and tried many times to keep Oxitec out of the state. Despite the backlash, city officials in the Florida Keys approved Oxitec to begin testing in the United States. Meanwhile, Intrexon has built a mosquito production facility in Brazil and might soon begin large-scale production.

Like Intrexon and its genetically modified male mosquitoes, other researchers have begun looking for ways to minimize the threat of *Aedes*

Genetically modified mosquitoes are bred in laboratories and are only released in specific areas for testing.

mosquitoes. Entomologist Scott O'Neil, dean of science at Monash University in Melbourne, Australia, has figured out a way to use naturally occurring *Wolbachia* bacteria to prevent mosquitoes from transmitting diseases. The technology was originally intended to prevent dengue, but O'Neil believes it will be effective against Zika as well. Aryn Baker of *TIME* magazine explained O'Neil's process:

> Like the beneficial bacteria that colonize the human gut, Wolbachia does not harm the insects it inhabits; instead it blocks the proliferation of harmful viruses, like dengue ...
>
> Wolbachia does not spread through the air, or via insect-to-insect contact. Instead, it is passed on from mother to offspring. When an insect has Wolbachia, the bacterium takes up residence in all of the cells, including a female's ovaries. That means all her progeny [children] will carry the bacteria, and her daughters will in turn pass it on to their offspring, and so on, until the bacteria spreads throughout the population. And the bacterium has

evolved a neat trick. If an infected male fertilizes
an uninfected female's eggs, they won't hatch.[36]

After years of failed attempts, O'Neil finally managed to transfer the bacteria into a mosquito embryo and from there, grew a colony of *Ae. aegypti* that are maintained in his lab and occasionally collected and released to test sites in Australia, Indonesia, Vietnam, Brazil, and Colombia as part of the Eliminate Dengue program. If these trials are successful, modified mosquitoes could be the answer to eliminating all mosquito-transmitted viruses, but it could be another decade before O'Neil's tests are completed.

It is often joked that humankind should step in and get rid of mosquitoes altogether. What do they do besides make people itchy and get them sick? According to some scientists, not much. In a discussion of *Ae. aegypti*, Dina Fonseca, a professor of entomology at Rutgers University, told National Public Radio (NPR), "I'm not worried about eradicating an invasive mosquito. It's an urban species that specializes on feeding on people. The result of removing them is health to humans and more people."[37] No animal that eats mosquitoes eats only one type, so the removal of one or two *Aedes* species would most likely not cause any huge ecological consequences. A UN Convention on Biological Diversity recently noted that 150 species go extinct every day anyway. "I think you could make a pretty good case," said David Magnus, director of Stanford University's Center for Biomedical Ethics. "As long as we're aware of the consequences of the change, it could be consistent with our obligations to being good stewards of the environment."[38] Although conservationists may object, it seems as if getting rid of the mosquitoes that carry Zika could be a real option in the future.

Infection Equals Immunity

As Zika continues to infect people, doctors hope more and more that Zika is like dengue and chikungunya and gives the infected lifelong immunity. Immunity to a disease occurs when the body's immune system reacts to it and successfully fights it off; later, if the host is exposed again, the immune system will remember the illness and be able to destroy it before it infects the host again. It is because of this reaction that researchers are able to find antibodies in the bloodstream to a virus that an individual may not have had for a while. When an outbreak happens, whole populations can gain immunity to a certain disease at the same time, a phenomenon called herd immunity. Immune populations can only become susceptible to infection again in two scenarios. The first is that the immunity is temporary, as some immunities tend to be. The second is that after a few years, children have inevitably been born into the population, but they do not have immunity like the rest of the community because they have never encountered the disease before. Such is the case with measles, an outbreak of which happens every two or three years and almost exclusively involves young kids. Recent studies suggest that Zika does, in fact, come with some level of immunity, although researchers are still trying to figure out how long that immunity might last.

The first study to prove that humans would likely develop immunity to Zika was an experiment on rhesus monkeys, the very same kind that first alerted Alexander Haddow to the disease. Researchers at the University of Wisconsin infected eight monkeys, including two pregnant ones, with the Asian strain of Zika, the one found in Brazil. The six nonpregnant monkeys showed traces of the disease in their blood for up to ten days and traces in their urine and saliva for up to seventeen days. The two pregnant monkeys, however, had the disease for much longer, and the researchers took that to mean the mother and child were cyclically infecting each other. After all the monkeys had been cleared of the disease, it appeared they were immune, having been infected again ten weeks later and showing no traces of the disease.

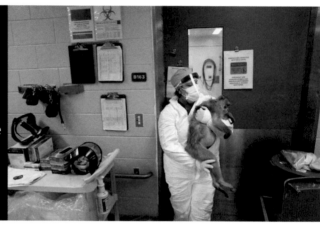

Studies have shown that pregnant rhesus monkeys retain the Zika virus for much longer than usual, suggesting that prolonged exposure to the virus may be the cause of microcephaly.

The truth of the matter is that experts will not really know how long the immunity to Zika lasts until someone who previously contracted the disease contracts it again. The WHO is more conservative in its estimations of possible lifelong immunity because there is no way to test how long immunity will last in a lab. "Experts who advise WHO and have closely followed the dramatic resurgence of dengue and the recent transformation of chikungunya into an international threat are reluctant to issue reassuring advice concerning the potential of epidemic Zika virus strains to spread beyond the Americas," said an article on the WHO website. "Outbreaks of dengue are now recurring in countries at short intervals, suggesting it is unlikely that Zika will simply burn itself out and go away. Moreover, flaviviruses are well-equipped to adapt to ecological pressures and exploit opportunities to spread."[39] Other reports suggest Zika may die out in three years for at least a decade, depending on how long immunity lasts. If that were to happen, it would give the medical community time to develop a vaccine before another wave of Zika crashes down.

Creating a Vaccine

Many drug companies leapt at the chance to be the one to manufacture a vaccine for Zika, but now, only two seem promising and have begun human trials. The first is the ZPIV vaccine. ZPIV is a traditional kind of vaccine, a "killed" one. According to NBC News,

> *To develop the vaccine, researchers kill the virus with chemicals, leaving behind harmless proteins that the body can learn to recognize as foreign invaders. Using those proteins as targets, the immune system can then produce antibodies to latch onto live virus particles and destroy them. This kind of vaccine is much safer than ones that depend on live virus particles to foster immunity.*[40]

Although it is a reliable type of vaccine that performed well in monkey trials, ZPIV may take

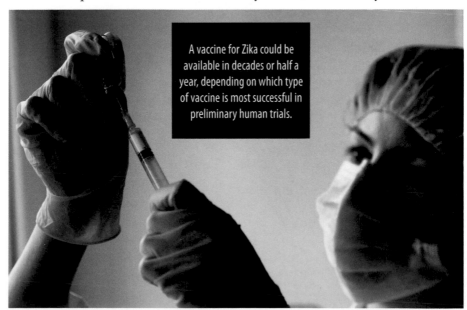

A vaccine for Zika could be available in decades or half a year, depending on which type of vaccine is most successful in preliminary human trials.

decades to perfect for human use, making it hard to treat Zika in the here and now. In the future, it could help, but it is most likely not the solution doctors are looking for.

The second vaccine is more experimental in the way it functions. Developed by Dr. Anthony Fauci's team at the NIH, it uses viral DNA to give immunity. The *New York Times* explained,

> *[The process] involves manufacturing a harmless piece of the virus's DNA, the molecule that acts like an instruction manual for the body. Once inject-ed, the DNA tells human cells to make Zika pro-teins. Those proteins then assemble themselves in harmless viruslike particles that trick the body into developing antibodies that can fight the disease if it arrives.*[41]

Using this technique, Fauci's team had a vaccine in weeks. However, though the process is quick, this method of immunization has not been proven to work in humans. Although sometimes used in animals, no vaccine created in this way has been approved for use in humans before. Even if it is approved, people would be required to get multiple vaccinations since DNA-based vaccines require many doses to work. If it works, though, there could be a Zika vaccine as early as 2018. As of April 2017, it had moved to the second phase of testing, indicating that its first human trial was successful.

While drug makers are obviously compelled to find a vaccine for Zika for the sake of public health, profit is also a strong motivator. Because of Zika's high pro-file and because of the wealthy countries such as the United States and Brazil that it has infected, there is actually money to be made with a vaccine for it. Generally, tropical, mosquito-transmitted diseases are more common in poorer nations, making vaccines for them less profitable for drug manufacturers because they either have to sell them cheaply or risk not selling them at all. Zika is proving to be an exception, though.

Can Zika Be Useful?

In May 2017, *Japan Today* announced that British scientists were experimenting with using the Zika virus to fight brain cancer in adults, whose brains are not affected the same way developing babies' are:

> The research will focus on glioblastoma, the most common form of brain cancer, which has a five-year survival rate of barely 5 percent … In glioblastoma, the cancer cells are similar to those in the developing brain, suggesting that the virus could be used to target them while sparing normal adult brain tissue. Experts say existing treatments have to be given at low doses to avoid damaging healthy tissue.[1]

Only time and research will tell whether using Zika this way will be effective.

1. Kate Kelland, "Scientists to Test Whether Zika Can Kill Brain Cancer Cells," *Japan Today*, May 22, 2017. japantoday.com/category/features/health/scientists-to-test-whether-zika-can-kill-brain-cancer-cells.

Going the Way of Smallpox

The ultimate goal of public health is to eliminate diseases, or to reduce the number of infections to zero and no longer need intervention measures such as inoculation. In other words, experts hope they eventually will not even need a vaccine to keep the disease at bay anymore because there is no way for it to spread. The only human disease to ever be eradicated worldwide was smallpox in 1979, but doctors hope that many other diseases, including Zika, will someday join that list. Walter R. Dowdle, director of the Polio Antivirals Initiative at the Task Force for Global Health, had this to say about the characteristics of a disease that could be eradicated:

> *Three indicators were considered to be of primary importance: an effective intervention is available to interrupt transmission of the agent; practical*

diagnostic tools with sufficient sensitivity and specificity are available to detect levels of infection that can lead to transmission; and humans are essential for the life-cycle of the agent, which has no other vertebrate reservoir and does not amplify in the environment.[42]

The "effective intervention" to "interrupt transmission" of Zika could be as simple as a vaccine and some form of mosquito control used together to keep people from being infected. If a vaccine is created and distributed to everyone who needs it and mosquitoes are rendered unable to pass on the virus or carry it, then there will be no way for the disease to be spread since it leaves the system entirely after, at most, six months. The only issue here is that getting everyone vaccinated will require huge national campaigns and a lot of money, making it less likely that people in underprivileged countries will have complete access to the vaccine.

Although lab testing is already available, a new handheld device may be the perfect "practical diagnostic tool." Able to test for Zika using saliva, urine, or blood, the device changes color when Zika DNA is present in a sample. As an additional tool to lab analysis, the new device is portable, making it useful for diagnosing patients in remote areas and increasing

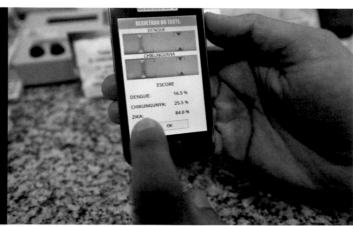

Advanced Zika testing procedures such as this one, which takes only 30 minutes, provide quick and accurate results that will help simplify identification and treatment of Zika on a global scale.

the number of cases medical professions can document. Having clearer statistics about Zika infection will help researchers better meet a community's needs and ultimately make it easier to track and prevent the disease's spread.

The one criterion for possible eradication that Zika does not meet is the one that states that humans should be essential for the virus to continue. Zika originated in primates, and the *Aedes* mosquitoes in the Zika Forest have actually been found to prefer to bite them. Zika, in short, does not need people, and that will make it harder or maybe impossible to eradicate it. Rendering mosquitoes unable to transmit the disease is really the only way researchers might be able defeat Zika entirely, since if mosquitoes cannot transmit it, then even primates will be protected from catching it. A species-wide change like that, however, could take a very, very long time.

The honest answer is that experts just do not know. Zika's cousins—yellow fever, dengue, and West Nile—have been hard to fight against because mosquito transmission has, until recently, been almost impossible to stop. With new mosquito control methods on the horizon, however, humanity may finally be able to overcome some of its oldest and newest viral enemies. Zika could be with us for a while, but it may not be with us forever.

Chapter One: Zika's World Tour

1. Mark R Duffy et al., "Zika Virus Outbreak on Yap Island, Federated States of Micronesia," *New England Journal of Medicine*, vol. 360, no. 24 (2009): 2537. www.nejm.org/doi/pdf/10.1056/NEJMoa0805715.

2. Jon Cohen, "Zika's Long, Strange Trip into the Limelight," *Science*, February 8, 2016. www.sciencemag.org/news/2016/02/zika-s-long-strange-trip-limelight.

3. Bahar Gholipour, "Zika Virus Was in Brazil a Year Before It Was Detected," Live Science, March 24, 2016. www.livescience.com/54161-when-did-zika-virus-enter-brazil.html.

4. Debra Goldschmidt, "Florida Health Officials Confirm Local Zika Transmission," CNN, July, 29, 2016. www.cnn.com/2016/07/29/health/florida-health-officials-confirm-local-zika-transmission/.

5. Associated Press, "Puerto Rico Reports First Death from Zika-Related Paralysis," *Guardian*, August 19, 2016. www.theguardian.com/world/2016/aug/19/puerto-rico-zika-virus-paralysis-death.

6. Chelsey Coombs, "The Zika Virus's Family Tree," *The Atlantic*, February 10, 2016. www.theatlantic.com/health/archive/2016/02/zika-yellow-fever-flaviviruses/462171/.

7. Elaine Schmidt, "UCLA Scientists Unravel the Genetic Evolution of Zika Virus," University of California, Los Angeles, April 15, 2016.

newsroom.ucla.edu/releases/ucla-scientists-un-ravel-the-genetic-evolution-of-zika-virus.

Chapter Two: Symptoms, Complications, Diagnosis, and Treatment

8. Samantha Olson, "Zika First Symptoms Facts and Myths 2016: Flu, Fever, Signs of Infection," *Medical Daily*, August 10, 2016. www.medicaldaily.com/zika-first-symptoms-facts-and-myths-2016-flu-fever-signs-infection-394513.

9. Heather Brannon, "What Are the Defining Features of a Maculopapular Rash?," VeryWell, February 28, 2016. www.verywell.com/maculo-papular-1068903.

10. "Zika and Guillain-Barré Syndrome," Centers for Disease Control and Prevention, August 9, 2016. www.cdcgov/zika/healtheffects/gbs-qa.html.

11. Thais dos Santos et al., "Zika Virus and the Guillain–Barré Syndrome—Case Series from Seven Countries," *New England Journal of Medicine*, vol. 375, no. 16, 2016, p. 1598. www.nejm.org/doi/pdf/10.1056/NE-JMc1609015.

12. "Microcephaly & Other Birth Defects," Centers for Disease Control and Prevention, January 5, 2017. www.cdc.gov/zika/healtheffects/birth_defects.html.

13. Quoted in Laura A. Stokowski, "More Than Microcephaly: Congenital Zika Syndrome," Medscape, September 21, 2016. www.medscape.com/viewarticle/868966_2.

14. Sonja A. Rasmussen et al., "Zika Virus and Birth Defects—Reviewing the Evidence for Causality," *New England Journal of Medicine*, vol. 374, no. 20, 2016, p. 1985. www.nejm.org/doi/pdf/10.1056/NEJMsr1604338.

15. "Only Some People Need Zika Testing," Centers for Disease Control and Prevention, July 28, 2016. www.cdc.gov/zika/pdfs/tested_for_zika_flyer.pdf.

16. Alexandra Sifferlin, "10 Zika Facts You Need to Know Now," *TIME*, May 4, 2016. time.com/4318624/zika-virus-and-birth-defects-what-you-need-to-know/.

Chapter Three: Transmission and Prevention

17. Rik Bleijs, "Zika Virus Transmission," Zika Virus Net. www.zikavirusnet.com/transmission.html.

18. Catherine Zettel and Phillip Kaufman, "Yellow Fever Mosquito—*Aedes aegypti* (Linnaeus)," University of Florida, April 2016. entnemdept.ufl.edu/creatures/aquatic/aedes_aegypti.htm#life.

19. Zettel and Kaufman, "Yellow Fever Mosquito."

20. "Route and Susceptibility: Mucous Membranes and Target Cells," NAM. www.aidsmap.com/Route-and-susceptibility-mucous-membranes-and-target-cells/page/1324028/.

21. "Zika and Sexual Transmission," Centers for Disease Control and Prevention, December 1, 2016. www.cdc.gov/zika/transmission/sexual-transmission.html.

22. Maryn McKenna, "It's Official: Zika Is a Sexually Transmitted Infection," *National Geographic*, August 1, 2016. news.

nationalgeographic.com/2016/08/zika-florida-travel-sex-cdc/.

23. Quoted in Judy Woodruff, "Why Is Zika Virus Spreading So Quickly?," PBS *NewsHour*, January 28, 2016. www.pbs.org/newshour/bb/why-is-zika-virus-spreading-so-quickly/.

Chapter Four: The Social Realities of Zika

24. Quoted in Jennifer Meckles, "Man Who Had Zika Virus Shares His Story," KSDK-TV, April 24, 2016. www.ksdk.com/news/local/as-state-health-officials-continue-to-monitor-the-zika-virus-one-man-is-sharing-his-story-of-first-hand-experience-with-the-/152203979.

25. Nick Brown, "For One Zika Patient, Lingering Symptoms and Few Answers," Reuters, September 12, 2016. www.reuters.com/article/us-health-zika-patient-insight-id USKCN11I0AT.

26. Brown, "For One Zika Patient, Lingering Symptoms and Few Answers."

27. Julie Beck, "The Importance of Contraception to the Zika Fight," *The Atlantic*, July 1, 2016. www.theatlantic.com/health/archive/2016/07/the-importance-of-contraception-to-the-zika-fight/489767/.

28. Beck, "The Importance of Contraception to the Zika Fight."

29. "News Update: Is Zika a Tipping Point in the Fight for Reproductive Rights in Latin America?," Global Fund for Women. www.globalfundforwomen.org/is-zika-a-tipping-point-for-reproductive-rights-in-latin-america/#.WH_Ij_krLIU.

30. Katherine Jinyi Li, "Brazil's Zika Mothers Are Speaking Out," *Seattle Globalist*, June 28, 2016. www.seattleglobalist.com/2016/06/28/brazil-zika-mothers-speaking-out/53007.

31. Candyce H. Stapen, "How Zika Virus Is Affecting Caribbean Travel," *Washington Post*, June 22, 2016. www.washingtonpost.com/lifestyle/travel/how-zika-virus-is-affecting-caribbean-travel/2016/06/21/d4f48e20-2f1b-11e6-9b37-42985f6a265c_story.html?utm_term=.9a526430fcd3.

32. Quoted in "Social and Economic Costs of Zika Can Reach Up to US$ 18 Billion in Latin America and the Caribbean," United Nations Development Programme, April 6, 2017. www.undp.org/content/undp/en/home/presscenter/pressreleases/2017/04/06/social-and-economic-costs-of-zika-can-reach-up-to-us-18-billion-in-latin-america-and-the-caribbean.html.

33. Quoted in Dennis Thompson, "Many Americans Are Dangerously Wrong about Zika Virus," CBS News, March 30, 2016. www.cbsnews.com/news/many-americans-are-dangerously-wrong-about-zika-virus/.

34. Paul Senatori, "Zika Virus: The Media Effect," MediaQuant, March 13, 2016. www.mediaquant.net/2016/03/the-zika-virus-the-media-affect/.

Chapter Five: Looking to the Future

35. Kate Tulenko, "Zika: The Cost of Doing Nothing," *Global Health and Diplomacy*, Spring 2016. onlinedigeditions.com/article/Zika%3A_The_Cost_Of_Doing_Nothing/2458978/298544/article.html.

36. Aryn Baker, "How Infecting Mosquitoes with a Bacterium Could Stop the Zika Virus," *TIME*, May 5, 2016. time.com/4319619/zika-virus-mosquitoes-wolbachia-technology/.

37. Malaka Gharib, "Would It Be a Bad Thing to Wipe Out a Species ... if It's a Mosquito?," NPR, February 20, 2016. www.npr.org/sections/goatsandsda/2016/02/20/467094440/would-it-be-a-bad-thing-to-wipe-out-a-species-if-its-a-mosquito.

38. Gharib, "Would It Be a Bad Thing to Wipe Out a Species ... if It's a Mosquito?"

39. "One Year into the Zika Outbreak: How an Obscure Disease Became a Global Health Emergency," World Health Organization. www.who.int/emergencies/zika-virus/articles/one-year-outbreak/en/index5.html.

40. Linda Carroll and Samuel Sarmiento, "'Striking' Results from Early Zika Vaccine Trial," NBC News, August 4, 2016. www.nbcnews.com/storyline/zika-virus-outbreak/striking-results-early-zika-vaccine-trial-n623016.

41. Katie Thomas, "The Race for a Zika Vaccine," *New York Times*, November 19, 2016. www.nytimes.com/2016/11/20/business/testing-the-limits-of-biotech-in-the-race-for-a-zika-vaccine.html.

42. Walter R. Dowdle, "The Principles of Disease Elimination and Eradication," *Morbidity and Mortality Weekly Report*, vol. 48, no. 1, 1999. www.cdc.gov/mmwr/preview/mmwrhtml/su48a7.htm.

GLOSSARY

antibody: A protein molecule produced by the immune system to destroy foreign particles such as viruses and infectious bacteria.

arthritis: The medical term for inflammation of the joints.

chikungunya: A viral infection spread by mosquitoes. Its symptoms are very similar to those of the Zika virus, but it does not cause microcephaly and is more widespread.

dengue fever: A mosquito-borne viral disease that can cause severe joint and muscle pain for an extended period.

endemic: Native to a certain place.

entomology: A branch of zoology that deals with insects.

epidemic: Spreading widely and affecting many individuals at one time.

immunoglobulin: The part of the blood containing antibodies.

inoculate: To vaccinate.

pandemic: A global disease outbreak.

vector: An organism that transmits an infectious particle.

virion: The part of a virus that transmits genetic code to host cells.

virus: An infectious agent that replicates only within the cells of living hosts.

ORGANIZATIONS TO CONTACT

Centers for Disease Control and Prevention (CDC)
1600 Clifton Road
Atlanta, GA 30329
(800) 232-4636
www.cdc.gov
A research division of the U.S. Department of Health and Human Services, the CDC offers information about the prevention and cure of infectious diseases that threaten the American public.

Foundation for Children with Microcephaly
21620 N. 26th Avenue, Suite #140
Phoenix, AZ 85027
(877) 476-5503
childrenwithmicro.org
help@childrenwithmicro.org
This nonprofit organization aims to educate people about how microcephaly affects individuals and families as well as provide support for those who have been diagnosed.

National Institutes of Health (NIH)
9000 Rockville Pike
Bethesda, MD 20892
(301) 496-4000
www.nih.gov
The NIH is a research facility focused on improving public health, lengthening life, and reducing the effects of illness and disability.

UNICEF
3 United Nations Plaza
New York, NY 10017
(212) 326-7000
www.unicef.org
Working with the United Nations, UNICEF provides
humanitarian programs for children and focuses on
youth health programs in times of disease outbreak.

World Health Organization (WHO)
Regional Office for the Americas
525 23rd Street N.W.
Washington, DC 20037
(202) 974-3000
www.who.int
The WHO works with governments all over the world
to combat disease and provides resources on the study of
diseases on a global scale.

FOR MORE INFORMATION

Books

Bickerstaff, Linda. *Your Immune System: Protecting Yourself Against Infection and Illness.* New York, NY: Rosen Central, 2011.
This book presents and explains the basics of the immune system and how it fights infections.

Edwards, Sue Bradford. *The Zika Virus.* Minneapolis, MN: ABDO, 2016.
This book takes a comprehensive look at the Zika virus from its origins to the 2015 outbreak, its effects, and the ways the medical community is trying to fight it.

Friedlander, Mark P. *Outbreak: Disease Detectives at Work.* Minneapolis, MN: Twenty-First Century Books, 2009.
The author gives a history of epidemics and the ways in which they have been stopped by medical science.

Jones, Phill. *Viruses.* New York, NY: Chelsea House, 2012.
This book examines the life cycle, effects, and mutation of viruses, as well as why they continue to be such a challenge to the medical community.

McNeil, Donald G., Jr. *Zika: The Emerging Epidemic.* New York, NY: W. W. Norton & Co., 2016.
This book gives a more advanced analysis of Zika's origins, spread, and coming solutions.

Shea, John M. *Viruses Up Close.* New York, NY: Gareth Stevens, 2014.
The author takes a look at how viruses can be spread so quickly, including information on virus replication and precautions against being infected.

Websites

American Academy of Pediatrics
www.aap.org
This website gives information about children's health, including developments surrounding Zika-related microcephaly.

Centers for Disease Control and Prevention (CDC)
www.cdc.gov/zika/index.html
This government website offers facts about Zika's health effects, travel warnings, and ways to protect against it.

National Institute of Allergy and Infectious Diseases
www.niaid.nih.gov/diseases-conditions/zika-virus
This website holds information about disease research and future solutions for Zika.

Pan American Health Organization
www.paho.org/hq
This website provides up-to-date information from the highest authorities on disease research and the development of the Zika epidemic.

Zika Virus Net
www.zikavirusnet.com
This website collects information from many sources, including news, literature, and international health groups, on Zika.

Michelle Denton is a recent graduate of Canisius College. She holds a bachelor's degree in English and creative writing and graduated cum laude from the All-College Honors Program. She lives in Buffalo, New York, where she works as props master at the Subversive Theatre Collective, and she is in the process of having her first stage play produced there. This is her second title for Lucent Press.